PLANNING YOUR
GARDEN

A PRACTICAL GUIDE TO DESIGNING AND PLANTING A GARDEN, WITH
15 PLANS AND OVER 200 INSPIRATIONAL PICTURES   PETER McHOY

southwater

This edition is published by Southwater, an imprint of Anness Publishing Ltd,
Blaby Road, Wigston, Leicestershire LE18 4SE; info@anness.com

www.southwaterbooks.com; www.annesspublishing.com

Anness Publishing has a new picture agency outlet for images for publishing, promotions
or advertising. Please visit our website www.practicalpictures.com for more information.

Publisher: Joanna Lorenz
Senior Editor: Caroline Davison
Designer: Ian Sandom
Production Controller: Wendy Lawson
Illustrator: Neil Bulpitt

© Anness Publishing Limited 2013

PUBLISHER'S NOTE
Although the advice and information in this book are believed to be accurate
and true at the time of going to press, neither the authors nor the publisher
can accept any legal responsibility or liability for any errors or omissions that
may have been made nor for any inaccuracies nor for any loss, harm or injury
that comes about from following instructions or advice in this book.

PAGE 1: A garden that is full of plants needs to
be carefully planned.
PAGE 2: A small garden can still incorporate a
wealth of different features.
PAGE 3: Paving can be softened by allowing the
plants to spill over the edge of the border.
PAGE 4: *Verbena*.
PAGE 5: *Narcissus jonquilla*.

CONTENTS

INTRODUCTION

Few of us are totally content with our gardens. Despite the immense pleasure we derive from them, there's always something that could be better. Most of us long for a larger garden, a few for something smaller and more manageable, but the vast majority of us have to make the best of our existing plot. Improving it, coaxing the maximum impact from it, is an enjoyable challenge that most of us would rise to – if only we knew how.

Gardening is about growing plants, but the setting in which we place them is probably the element that makes a garden appealing or otherwise. Tastes in gardening styles vary as much as in other aspects of living, and what appeals to one person may not appeal to another, but the test of a good garden design is whether it appeals to *you*. This book sets out to help you create a garden that reflects your taste, your personality.

It also lifts the lid on the magic box of imagination and inspiration. It shows you what other enthusiastic gardeners have done, and how others have made the most of sometimes unpromising plots. This is an eminently practical book, too, and it will guide you through drawing your first plans to planting and simple garden construction.

■ ABOVE
A garden that looks lived in will be used.

■ OPPOSITE
Paths and walls form a backdrop for plants.

Garden Planning Made Easy

....

You can have your garden designed and constructed by professionals, but it will cost a great deal of money, and the chances are that it won't give you as much satisfaction as having created a garden by your own efforts.

This chapter explains the basic techniques for simple garden design, but it's up to you as to how you interpret them and what you create with the tools provided. The remaining chapters are packed with inspirational ideas, but only you can decide what's right for your garden. Tastes in gardens vary as much as in interior decor and preferences in music or art. The acid test of whether your new design has worked is whether it pleases you.

Use the techniques suggested to experiment on paper – you will soon develop skills that will enable you to design your garden with confidence.

■ ABOVE
A striking garden, which uses water and paving in a highly structured design.

■ OPPOSITE
An informal, country-style garden, with colourful borders overflowing with
flowers and shrubs, yet with a clear sense of design.

TAKING STOCK

If you're planning and planting a new garden from a virgin plot of land, then your starting point is a wish list of features to incorporate. But if you are redesigning an existing garden, it's also important to decide whether there are features that you would like to retain.

Never let an existing feature dictate your new garden, unless you have no alternative but to work around it. For instance, you may be limited by what you can do with a large tree or unsightly garage. While you may not want the disruption of digging up the drive and moving the garage, don't be dictated to by the presence of ordinary garden paths. They may be tiring to lift, but a straight path down the centre of a narrow garden will limit your ability to be creative with your new design.

Make lists of what has to stay and what you want to work around and improve.

THE WISH LIST
Make your wish list before you attempt your design. It is unlikely to be fulfilled completely, but setting down those things that are a priority to you should ensure that the most important features are included.

Everyone has different preferences, so decide which features you regard as essential (it may be something as mundane as a clothes drier or as stimulating as a water feature), those that are important but less essential for your ideal garden, and those elements that you regard simply as desirable.

While designing your garden, keep in mind those features listed as essential. Try to incorporate as many of them as possible, but don't cram in so many that a strong sense of design is sacrificed.

It will immediately become apparent if the list of the most desirable features is not feasible within the limited space available, but you will probably be able to introduce some of the more important ones. However, attempt to include only those features ticked (checked) simply as desirable if you have space.

GARDEN PRIORITIES	Essential	Important	Desirable
Flowerbeds	[ ]	[ ]	[ ]
Herbaceous border	[ ]	[ ]	[ ]
Shrub border	[ ]	[ ]	[ ]
Trees	[ ]	[ ]	[ ]
Lawn	[ ]	[ ]	[ ]
Gravelled area	[ ]	[ ]	[ ]
Paved area/patio	[ ]	[ ]	[ ]
Built-in barbecue	[ ]	[ ]	[ ]
Garden seats/furniture	[ ]	[ ]	[ ]
Rock garden	[ ]	[ ]	[ ]
Pond	[ ]	[ ]	[ ]
Other water feature	[ ]	[ ]	[ ]
Wildlife area	[ ]	[ ]	[ ]
Greenhouse/conservatory	[ ]	[ ]	[ ]
Summerhouse	[ ]	[ ]	[ ]
Tool shed	[ ]	[ ]	[ ]
Fruit garden	[ ]	[ ]	[ ]
Herb garden	[ ]	[ ]	[ ]
Vegetable garden	[ ]	[ ]	[ ]
Trellis/pergola/arch	[ ]	[ ]	[ ]
Sandpit/play area	[ ]	[ ]	[ ]
Clothes drier/line	[ ]	[ ]	[ ]
Dustbin (trash can)	[ ]	[ ]	[ ]
Compost heap	[ ]	[ ]	[ ]
. . . .	[ ]	[ ]	[ ]
. . . .	[ ]	[ ]	[ ]
. . . .	[ ]	[ ]	[ ]
. . . .	[ ]	[ ]	[ ]
. . . .	[ ]	[ ]	[ ]
. . . .	[ ]	[ ]	[ ]
. . . .	[ ]	[ ]	[ ]

■ OPPOSITE
The initial sketch can be simple and need contain only the basic dimensions. Do not bother with anything that you do not intend to include in the new garden.

SURVEYING AND MEASURING

It is much better – and less expensive – to make your mistakes on paper first, rather than in the garden itself. Start by making a sketch of the garden as it is, and then work up your ideas.

If your garden is large, divide it into sections that can be pieced together later, but for a small garden the whole area will go on to a single sheet of paper. Leave space around the edge for measurements.

Write down the measurements of all the main features such as a tree, path or garage. Do not include anything that you are already sure you will not retain. Small rectangular gardens are very easy to measure. Sometimes the

boundary can be calculated simply by counting fence panels and multiplying up the length of a fence panel and post. Most other features can be fixed by measuring at right angles from the boundary.

If the shape of the garden is more complicated, it is usually possible to determine a position by laying a piece of string at right angles from the known straight edge, then measuring at right angles from this line.

WHAT YOU WILL NEED

■ A 30m (100ft) tape measure – preferably plasticized fabric as this is easy to work with but does not stretch.

■ A 1.8m (6ft) steel rule for short measurements.

■ Pegs to mark out positions, and to hold one end of the tape in position (meat skewers can be used to hold the end of the tape).

■ Pencils, sharpener and eraser.

■ Clipboard with graph paper.

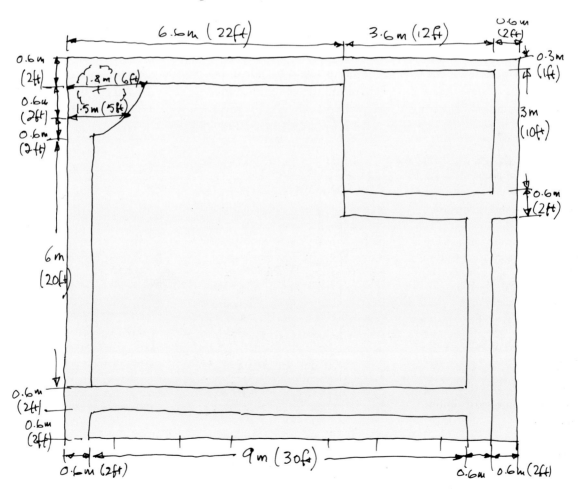

PUTTING THE PLAN ON PAPER

The exciting part of redesigning a garden comes when the basic structure is on the drawing board and you can start to work magical transformations as you try to test your ideas. Drawing to scale is the next step to reach this goal.

With the rough sketch from the garden drawn accurately to scale, the stimulating part of garden planning can begin. It is when dreams can start to be translated into reality. Making an accurate scale drawing of your existing garden is an essential starting point if you want to simplify the design work that follows.

The rough sketch must be transferred to a scale drawing before any detailed plans can be sketched out. Drawing it to scale will help you to calculate the amount of any paving required, and also enable you to tailor beds, borders and lawns to sizes that will involve the least amount of cutting of hard materials such as paving slabs or bricks.

Use graph paper for your scale drawing. Pads are adequate for a small garden or a section of a larger one, but if your garden is big, buy a large sheet (available from art and stationers' shops).

Use a scale that enables you to fit the plan on to your sheet of graph paper (or several taped together). For most small gardens, a scale of 1:50 (2cm to 1m or ¼in to 1ft) is about right; for a large garden, however, 1:100 (1cm to 1m or ⅛in to 1ft) might be better.

Draw the basic outline of the garden and the position of the house first, including the position of any doors and windows if relevant. Then add all the major features that you are likely to retain. You should have all the necessary measurements on the freehand sketch that you made in the garden.

Omit any features that you are sure will be eliminated from the new design, to keep it as uncluttered as possible. In this example, the summerhouse has been drawn in because it was considered to be in a good position and would be difficult to move. Although the corner tree was removed in the final design, it was included at this stage as a different design might have made use of it.

USING YOUR PLAN

1 Even expert designers make a number of rough sketches of possible designs before finalizing the chosen one, so devise a way of using your master outline again and again without having to keep redrawing it. One way is to make a number of photocopies or use tracing paper.

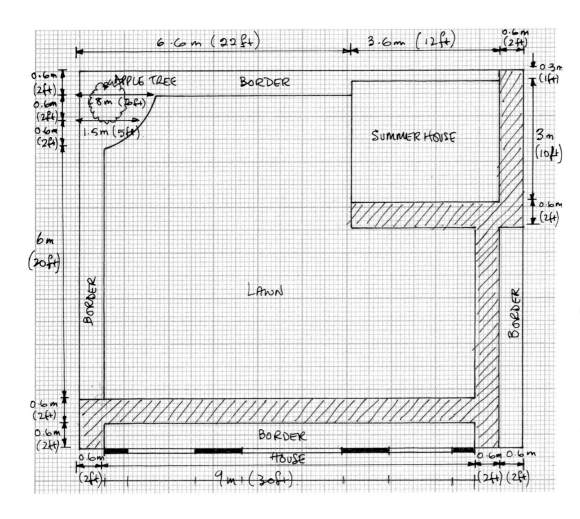

6·6 m (22 ft)　　3·6m (12 ft)　0·6m (2ft)

0·6m (2ft)
0·6m (2ft)
0·6m (2ft)

APPLE TREE　　BORDER

·8 m (2 ft)

1·5m (5 ft)

SUMMER HOUSE

0·3m (1 ft)

3 m (10 ft)

0·6m (2ft)

6 m (20ft)

BORDER

LAWN

BORDER

0·6 m (2ft)
0·6 m (2ft)

BORDER

0·6m (2ft)

HOUSE

9 m (30 ft)

0·6m (2ft)　0·6 m (2ft)

0·6m 0·6 m

■ LEFT
Using the information included on the freehand sketch made in the garden, draw a scale version that you can use during the design process. You may find it helpful to use graph paper.

2 If you have a drawing board, simply use tracing paper overlays for your roughs while experimenting with ideas. If you do not have a drawing board and your garden is small, you may be able to use a clipboard to hold the tracing paper firmly in position.

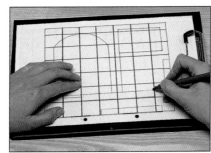

3 Film and pens of the type used for overhead projection sheets are effective if you prefer to use colours that can easily be wiped off for correction.

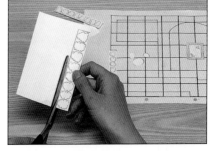

4 Try drawing and cutting out scale features that you want to include in your finished design, such as a raised pond, patio furniture or raised beds. These can be moved around until they look right, but they should be used as aids only once the overall design has been formulated in your mind. If you try to design your garden around the few key symbols that you have placed, it will almost certainly lack coherence.

CREATING YOUR DESIGN

The difficult part of redesigning or improving your garden is making a start. Once you start drawing, the ideas are sure to flow, especially if you have other gardens in mind that you like and can use as inspiration and a starting point. Don't attempt to copy someone else's plan in detail – it probably won't fit the size or style of your property, or your requirements – but such plans are excellent to refer to for inspiration when developing your own design.

If you decide on a garden with strong lines, rather than irregular flowering borders, it is worth deciding on whether you are going to plan a rectangular or diagonal or circular design. Any of these can be adapted to suit the size of your garden, and in the case of the circular pattern you might want to include overlapping circles. Where circles join, try to make any transitional curves gradual rather than abrupt. Whichever you choose, draw a grid on top of your plan to aid design (see opposite page). In a small garden surrounded by fencing, it can be useful to base the rectangular and diagonal grids on the spacing of fence posts – usually about 1.8m (6ft) apart.

A rectangular grid has been used in the example opposite, but as part of the trial-and-error phase it is worth trying different grids. A diagonal grid is often effective where the house is set in a large garden with plenty of space at the sides. The patio can be positioned at a 45-degree angle at the corner of the house, for example.

The size and shape of the garden will usually dictate the best grid, but if in doubt, try the other possibilities to see which one is most appropriate.

Bear in mind that many excellent, prize-winning gardens are created without such a grid, and sometimes these have, to some extent, evolved in a more flowing manner, developing feature by feature. Grids may help you, but do not hesitate to adopt a more freestyle approach if this comes more naturally.

LOOKING FOR INSPIRATION

Don't despair if inspiration does not come easily, or initial attempts seem disappointing. If you try these tips, you will almost certainly produce workable plans that you will be pleased with:

■ Look through books and magazines to decide which style of garden you like: formal or informal; the emphasis on plants or on hard landscaping; mainly foliage, texture and ground cover or lots of colourful flowers; straight edges or curved and flowing lines.

■ With the style decided, look at as many garden pictures as possible and for design ideas that appeal. Do not be influenced by individual plants; these can be changed.

■ Choose a grid, if applicable, and draw this on to your plan. This will help you think ideas through on logical lines.

■ Start sketching lots of designs but do not attempt to perfect them at this stage. Just explore ideas.

■ Do not concern yourself with planning planting schemes at this stage – concentrate on patterns and lines.

■ Do not spend time drawing in paving patterns or choosing materials yet.

■ Make a short list of those overall outlines that you like best. Then forget them for a day. It pays to take a fresh look at things after a short break.

■ If you still like one of your original roughs, begin work on that, filling in details like paving, surface textures such as gravel, and the position of focal point plants, etc. Don't include any planting plans at this stage.

■ If your original roughs lack appeal when you look at them again, repeat the process with another batch of ideas. You will probably see ways of improving some of your earlier efforts, so things will be easier this time around.

■ If you find it difficult to visualize sizes, peg the design out at full size on the ground with string, then modify the layout and your plan if necessary.

BEGIN THE DESIGN

1 Draw in any existing features to be retained (in this example the summerhouse), and the chosen grid (unless you want an informal style where a grid may be inappropriate). Use a different colour for the grid lines, to prevent the plan becoming cluttered and confused.

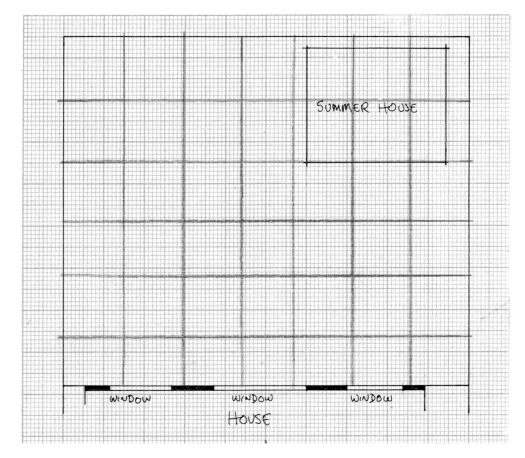

2 Use overlays (or photocopies) to experiment with a range of designs. Even if the first attempt looks satisfactory, try a number of variations. You can always come back to your first idea if it turns out to be the best one.

At this stage, do not include details such as patio furniture or individual plants (except for key focal-point plants and important trees or shrubs). When you have a design that you like, pencil in things like patio furniture (or use scale cut-out features if you prefer).

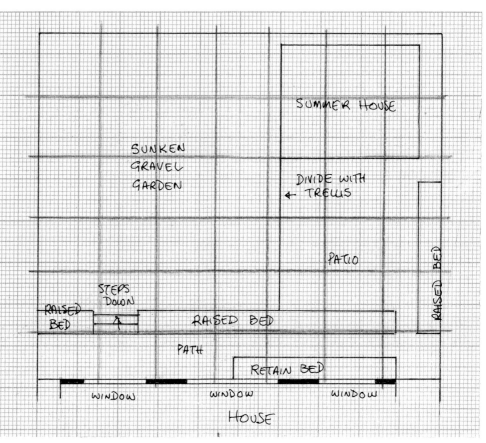

BASIC PATTERNS

Having decided on the style of garden that you want, and the features that you need to incorporate, it's time to tackle the much more difficult task of applying the theory to your own garden.

STARTING POINTS
The chances are that your garden will be the wrong size or shape, or the situation or outlook inappropriate to the style of garden that you have admired. The way around this impasse is to keep in mind a style without attempting to recreate it closely.

If you can't visualize the whole of your back or front garden as, say, a stone or Japanese garden, it may be possible to include the feature as an element within a more general design.

If you analyse successful formal garden designs, most fall into one of the three basic patterns described here, though clever planting and variations on the themes almost always result in individual designs.

■ **RIGHT**
CIRCULAR THEMES These are effective at disguising the predictable shape of a rectangular garden. Circular lawns, patios and beds are all options, and you only need to overlap and interlock a few circles to create a stylish garden. Plants fill the gaps between curved areas and straight edges.

Using a pair of compasses, try various combinations of circles to see whether you can create an attractive pattern. Be prepared to vary the radii and to overlap the circles if necessary.

■ **OPPOSITE LEFT DIAGONAL THEMES** This device creates a sense of space by taking the eye along and across the garden. Start by drawing grid lines at 45 degrees to the house or main fence. Then draw in the design, using the grid as a guide.

■ **OPPOSITE RIGHT RECTANGULAR THEMES** This is a popular choice, and many garden plans end up with a rectangular theme – even though there may have been no conscious effort to do so. The device is effective if you want to create a formal look, or wish to divide up a long, narrow garden into smaller sections.

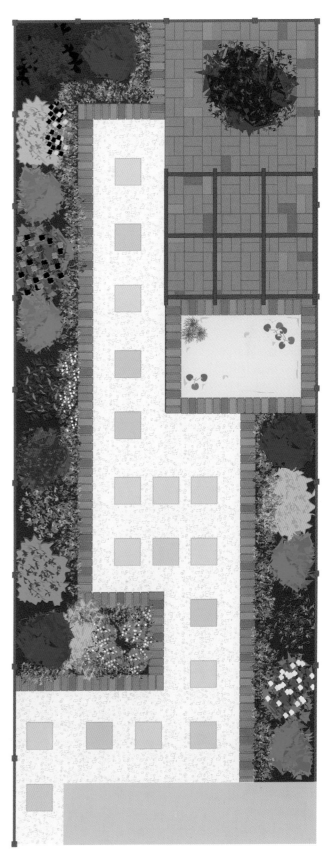

FORMAL AND INFORMAL

If you like straight lines and everything neat and clearly done to a plan, a formal garden should please, but for some gardeners an informal, more casual style that looks more like a simple setting for plants is likely to have more appeal. Informal gardens are also more adaptable to family use, with the lawn providing opportunities for play as well as relaxation for adults.

It's important to decide at an early stage whether the formal designs represented by some of the grids described earlier are right for your style of gardening, or even whether they fit your lifestyle – a growing family may prefer a more casual style of garden. Those who are interested in flowers and foliage rather than hard landscaping are more likely to feel at home among sweeping borders, hidden paths, and seats tucked into arbours or overlooking a wildlife pond.

Anyone who loves the informality of cottage gardens, which may be little more than a couple of borders either side of a path or lawn, may find a very structured garden unappealing. With informal gardens, it is the positioning of plants that gives it gardener appeal. Even the style of planting may be less planned, with self-sown seedlings coming up between other plants in the border, or among the paving.

If this is your kind of garden, follow your instinct, but remember that focal points and flowing curves are still important. Arbours, pergolas and ornaments, well-positioned garden seats, and a sense of overall planning and good planting sense are just as relevant in this kind of garden as in a more structured one.

■ RIGHT AND OPPOSITE
These two designs show how different a garden of the same size can look depending on whether a formal or informal style is used. Deciding on the degree of formality in the design comes early in the planning stage.

KEY TO PLAN

1 Ornament (on plinth)
2 Herb garden
3 Shed
4 Trellis
5 Climbers (e.g. ivy, parthenocissus and clematis) against trellis
6 Sundial or birdbath
7 Mixed border
8 Large pot with shrubs/shaped clipped box
9 Garden bench
10 Pool with fountain
11 Arch
12 Group of large shrubs
13 Screen-block wall
14 Patio furniture
15 Vegetable garden
16 Trellis arch
17 Path
18 House

INFORMALITY

■ BELOW

The planting here gives the impression of informality, but the symmetry of the design is formal.

KEY TO PLAN

1 Garden bench
2 Lawn
3 Herbaceous plants and bulbs
4 Shrubs
5 Thymes and other aromatic herbs planted between crazy paving
6 White metal garden bench
7 Pond
8 Bog garden
9 Red-stemmed dogwood
10 Dwarf conifers and heathers
11 Birdbath or sundial, with plants around base
12 Tree
13 House

UNUSUAL SHAPES

It may be possible to turn a problem shape to your advantage by using its unusual outline to create a garden that stands out from others in the street. Because of its originality, what was once a difficult area to plant will soon become the object of other gardeners' envy. The seven designs shown here illustrate how difficult sites can, with imagination and some careful planning, produce promising gardens.

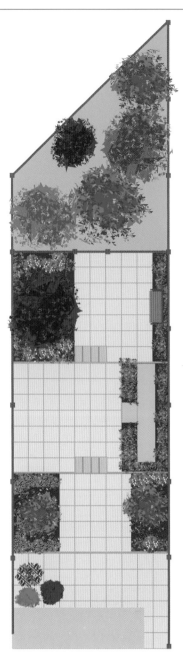

■ ABOVE
LONG AND TAPERING If the garden is long and pointed, try screening off the main area, leaving a gateway or arch to create the impression of more garden beyond while not revealing the actual shape. The tapering end of the garden could be used as an orchard, as here, or a vegetable garden.

Staggering the three paved areas, with small changes of level, adds interest. At the same time, a long view has been retained to give the impression of size.

■ ABOVE LEFT AND ABOVE CENTRE
LONG AND NARROW The plan on the left shows a design based on a circular theme. The paved area near the house can be used as a patio, and the one at the far end for drying the washing, largely out of sight from the house. Alternatively, if the end of the garden receives more sun, reverse the roles of the paved areas. Taking the connecting path across the garden at an angle, and using small trees or large shrubs to prevent the eye travelling straight along the sides, creates the impression of a garden to be explored. The plan on the right shows the use of diagonals to achieve a similar effect.

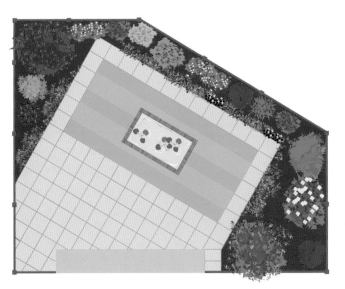

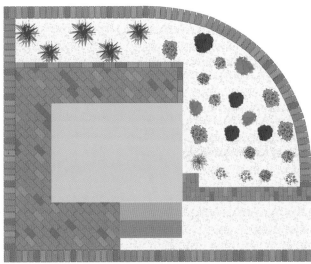

■ ABOVE
ANGULAR CORNER SITE Corner sites are often larger than other plots in the same road, and offer scope for some interesting designs. This one has been planned to make the most of the extra space at the side of the house, which has become the main feature of the garden instead of the more usual back or front areas.

■ ABOVE
CURVED CORNER SITE Curved corner gardens are more difficult to design effectively. In this plan the house is surrounded by a patio on the left-hand side, and a low wall partitions the patio from the rest of the garden, making it more private. For additional interest, a path separates the drive from the gravel garden. Gravel and boulders, punctuated by striking plants such as phormiums and yuccas, effectively marry the straight edges with the bold curve created by the corner site.

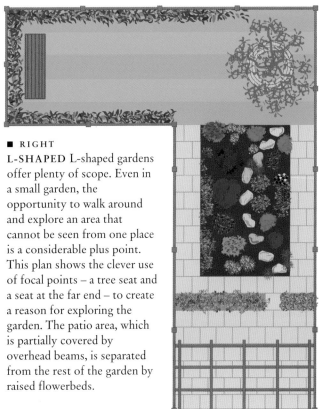

■ ABOVE
SQUARE AND SQUAT A small square site like this offers little scope for elaborate design, so keep to a few simple elements. To give the impression of greater space the viewpoint has been angled diagonally across the garden. For additional interest, the timber decking is slightly raised, creating a change of level. A small lawn can be difficult to cut in a tiny garden, but you could try an alternative to grass, such as chamomile, which needs trimming only infrequently.

The diagonal theme helps to counter the basic rectangular shape of the garden and makes the most of available space.

■ RIGHT
L-SHAPED L-shaped gardens offer plenty of scope. Even in a small garden, the opportunity to walk around and explore an area that cannot be seen from one place is a considerable plus point. This plan shows the clever use of focal points – a tree seat and a seat at the far end – to create a reason for exploring the garden. The patio area, which is partially covered by overhead beams, is separated from the rest of the garden by raised flowerbeds.

21

COPING WITH SLOPES

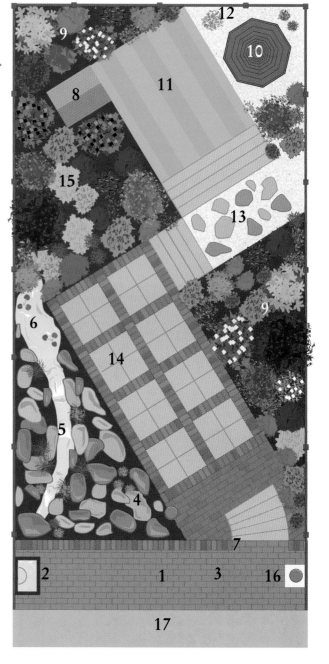

Sloping sites are particularly difficult to plan on paper, and they are much more challenging to design in general than flat sites. As sloping gardens vary so much in the degree of slope – whether the garden slopes down from the house or upwards – as well as size and aspect, it is also more difficult to adapt designs created by others. Although sloping gardens are difficult to design, the drawbacks can be turned into advantages. Changes of level can add interest and provide an excellent setting for rock gardens and cascading "streams".

KEY TO PLAN

1 Patio
2 Wall fountain with small pool
3 Bricks or clay pavers
4 Rock garden bank sloping downhill and towards a flat paved area
5 "Stream" with cascades
6 Pond, disappearing behind shrubs
7 Small retaining wall
8 Shed for tools and mower
9 Shrubs
10 Summerhouse with views across garden and attractive view below garden
11 Lawn
12 Gravel with alpines
13 Gravel area with natural paving
14 Pavers mixed with paving slabs
15 Trees and shrubs
16 Ornament (on plinth)
17 House

■ **ABOVE RIGHT**
SLOPING DOWN A downward-sloping garden with an attractive view is much easier to design successfully than an upward-sloping one. If the outlook is unattractive, however, it may be advisable to screen the lowest part of the garden with shrubs and small trees and use it as the main sitting area.

This plan demonstrates several important principles when designing a sloping garden, and unusually combines terraces with a natural slope. Terracing is expensive and time-consuming: it involves earth-moving, and retaining

walls on strong foundations have to be built. Moving the topsoil from one area to lower down the slope is unsatisfactory as part of the garden will be left with subsoil at the surface for planting – a recipe for disappointment. Topsoil should be set aside, the ground levelled, and then the topsoil returned, which is labour-intensive.

Terracing provides flat areas on which to walk and relax, and this design includes flat areas along the length of the garden. As these have been used for hard surfaces, the problem of subsoil and topsoil does not arise. Retaining the

natural slope for a large part of the garden reduces the amount of structural work required and cost.

Although there are some retaining walls, the two walls that zigzag down the garden are stepped so that they remain just above the surrounding ground.

Retaining a large area of naturally sloping ground also provides an ideal setting for rock outcrops and an artificial stream with a series of cascades.

Taking a path across the garden at an angle makes it seem less steep. A path that runs in a straight line down the slope only serves to emphasize the drop.

If the slope falls away from the house suddenly, building a raised patio like this will provide a level area and avoid the use of steps immediately outside the door.

■ RIGHT

SLOPING UPWARDS An upward slope is a challenge. Distant views are not a possibility, and even upper floors may look out on to a bank. Terracing in this situation can look oppressive, but a "secret" garden full of meandering paths flanked by shrubs is an effective way of dealing with the slope. Some retaining walls are usually necessary, but if planted with shrubs, the effect will be masked and the plants on the lower terraces will hide the upper walls and banks.

Lawns are difficult to accommodate on a steeply sloping site, and difficult to mow too, as mowers are awkward to carry up steps and steep ramps for access. It is generally best to avoid grass lawns, but use a grass "alternative" in a small levelled area. Chamomile and thyme require only an occasional trim with shears, which for a small area is not an onerous job.

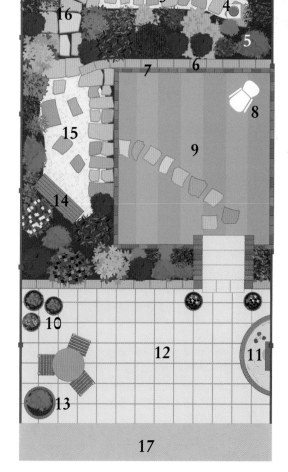

KEY TO PLAN

1 Small tree	9 Thyme or chamomile lawn
2 Shrubs	10 Plants in containers
3 Natural stone paving slabs set in gravel	11 Wall fountain with small pool beneath
4 Ornament on plinth as a focal point	12 Patio
5 Dwarf shrubs on bank	13 Shrub or small tree in large tub
6 Retaining wall	14 Seat
7 Brick edge	15 Natural stone paving set in gravel
8 Lounger or deckchair	16 Natural stone path
	17 House

FRONT GARDENS

Front gardens have special problems – especially if they have to accommodate a drive for the car. Perhaps for that reason they frequently lack interest and look uninspiring, yet it's the front garden that visitors see first, so it's worth making a special effort to create a good impression. Even enthusiastic gardeners with delightful back gardens are often let down by a dull front garden. Here two small front gardens with typical problems have been transformed by a little creative thinking and careful planning.

COUNTRY COTTAGE LOOK
Gardens don't come much more uninspired than this: a concrete drive, a small narrow flowerbed on the paved patio in front of the window, a narrow border along the edge of the garden, and a single flowering cherry tree placed in the centre of a rectangular lawn. However, the solution for this garden was a simple one, as the redesigned garden on the right shows. The cottage-garden style includes plants of all kinds which grow and mingle happily together with minimum intervention.

Besides being a short cut to the front door, the stepping stones encourage exploration of the garden and its plants. You actually walk through the planting, which cascades and tumbles around the paving slabs. The garden design has been reversed, with plants forming the heart of the garden rather than being peripherals around the edge. Don't be afraid to dig up a lawn – you can retain the year-round colour by planting evergreen shrubs and seasonal flowers.

PROBLEMS
▪ Although the cherry is spectacular in flower, and provides a show of autumn colour, it is attractive for only a few weeks of the year. Its present position precludes any major redesign, so it is best removed.
▪ Unclothed wooden fences contribute to the drab appearance.
▪ Small flowerbeds like these lack impact, and are too small for the imaginative use of shrubs or herbaceous perennials.

SOLUTIONS
▪ The lawn and tree have been removed, and the whole area planted with a mixture of dwarf shrubs, herbaceous perennials, hardy annuals, and lots of bulbs for spring interest.
▪ Stepping stones have been provided for those who want to take a short cut (they also make access for weeding easier).
▪ The fences have been replaced by low walls to make the garden appear less confined.

IMPACT WITH PRIVACY

Being on a corner, this garden is a jumble of shapes and angles, and as originally constructed lacks any sense of design. With its new look, the old curved path has been retained because its thick concrete base and the drain inspection cover within it would have made it difficult to move, but all the other lines have been simplified and more appropriate plants used. The curved, flowing stream along the right-hand side adds movement and sound to the garden.

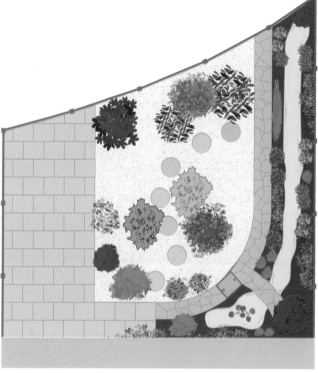

PROBLEMS

■ The bed along the left-hand side was a rock garden, but rock gardens are seldom successful on a flat site in a small garden.

■ The tree would have grown large, eventually casting considerable shade and dominating the garden.

■ Small beds like this, used for seasonal bedding, are colourful in summer but can lack interest in winter. This curve sits uneasily with the straight edge at one end and the curve of the path at the other.

SOLUTIONS

■ The rock garden has been paved so that the cultivated area is not divided by the drive.

■ Gravel replaces the lawn. This requires minimal maintenance and acts as a good foil for the plants.

■ Dwarf and medium-sized conifers create height and cover, and therefore a degree of privacy. Using species and varieties in many shades of green and gold, and choosing a range of shapes, makes this part of the garden interesting throughout the year.

■ Stepping stones add further interest. Because it isn't possible to see where the stepping stones lead to from either end (the conifers hide the route), a sense of mystery is added which tempts the visitor to explore.

■ The existing path has been retained but covered with slate crazy paving to make it more interesting.

■ A pond creates a water feature and also attracts wildlife.

■ The awkward, narrow curving strip has been turned into a stream with circulating water flowing over a cascade into the pond at one end.

■ LEFT
Instead of a lawn with a few flowerbeds around the edge, this small front garden has been planted in cottage-garden style. It is packed with interest throughout the year.

CREATING ILLUSIONS

Sometimes it's good to deceive – at least deceive the eye into thinking your garden is bigger or better than it really is! Try some of these simple devices to solve some of those difficult problems. The few simple forms of visual deception described here should enable you to make your garden look larger than it really is, helping to distract the eye from unattractive features by making the most of the positive.

■ RIGHT
First impressions here are of a large garden extending beyond the arch, yet it's an illusion done with a mirror!

■ ABOVE LEFT AND ABOVE RIGHT
A small garden will seem box-like if the boundary is clearly visible, especially if it is plain and man-made like a fence or a wall, and the boundary will dominate. Simply adding a narrow border with masking shrubs will not help because the boundary, although better clothed, will still be obvious. Bringing the border into the garden in broad sweeps, with a hint of the lawn disappearing behind a sweep towards the end of the garden, will blur the boundaries, giving the impression of more garden beyond.

■ ABOVE LEFT AND ABOVE RIGHT

Straight lines can be uncompromising, and a dominant feature at the end of a straight path will foreshorten the visual appearance. Curving the path slightly, and perhaps tapering it a little towards the end, will create the illusion of greater depth. If the focal point is also diminished in height or stature, the optical illusion will be increased.

■ ABOVE LEFT AND ABOVE RIGHT

A long, straight path will take the eye to the boundary unless the garden is very large, so try to introduce a feature that will arrest the eye part of the way along the path. A curve around an ornament, a large shrub or small tree will keep the eye within the garden. If you do not want to move an existing path, try erecting an arch over it, planted with an attractive climber to soften the outline and perhaps extended along the length of trellis on either side.

PREPARING A PLANTING PLAN

The hard landscaping described so far in this chapter acts like a skeleton and gives the garden structure, but it is the choice of plants that gives shape and character to a garden. It's important to think about structure first, but getting the planting plan right is equally important if your garden is to have real impact throughout the year.

CREATING THE OUTLINE

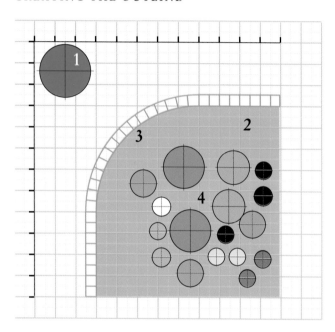

Start with the outline of the area to be planted, with distances marked on the graph paper to make positioning easier. Some good plant catalogues and books include plenty of pictures, and give likely heights and spreads for the plants. Treat heights and spreads with caution, however, as much depends on where you live, as well as on climate, soil and season.

If your plant knowledge is good, you may be able to draw directly on to your border plan, but if you find it easier to move around pieces of paper than use a pencil and eraser, cut out shapes to represent the plants that you are planning to include. Write on their height, spread and flowering period if this helps, and indicate their name on the back. Try colouring them, perhaps using stripes for variegated plants, and using green for evergreens. This will help form an overall picture.

KEY TO PLAN

1 Existing flagpole cherry (*Prunus* 'Amanogawa')
2 Lawn
3 Mowing edge
4 Cut-out plant symbols to position in border

ADDING THE PLANTS

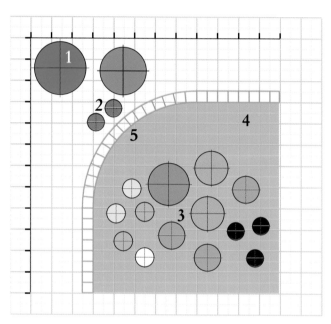

Position the symbols on your plan, starting with tall or key plants. It may be necessary to adjust them as other plants are added, but it is important that the key focal-point plants are well positioned as they will probably dominate the bed or border. Bear in mind the flowering periods, and ensure that evergreens are well distributed rather than clumped together, leaving large areas that will be bare in winter.

KEY TO PLAN

1 Existing flagpole cherry (*Prunus* 'Amanogawa')
2 Plants in position
3 Plants still to be positioned
4 Lawn
5 Mowing edge

FILLING OUT THE DESIGN

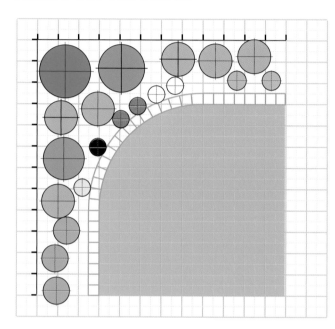

COMPLETING THE DESIGN

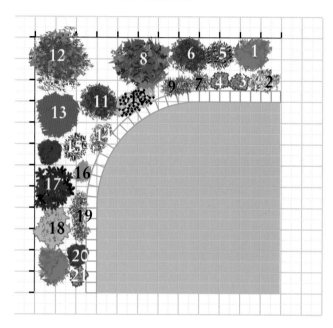

After placing the key plants, including tall ones best placed towards the back of the border, add the mid-height plants, but make sure some of these appear to drift towards the back of the border between the taller ones, to avoid a rigid, tiered effect. Finally, fill in with low-growing plants. The larger the drift of these, the more effective they are likely to be. Individual small plants often lack impact, and can be swamped by more vigorous neighbours.

The initial plans can be fairly crude as they merely explore the possibilities of various combinations and associations. To visualize the final effect more easily, draw your final planting plan in more detail.

KEY TO COMPLETING THE DESIGN PLAN

1 *Perovskia atriplicifolia* 90cm/3ft
2 Bergenia (evergreen) 30cm/1ft
3 *Diascia barberae* 30cm/1ft
4 *Houttuynia cordata* 'Chameleon' 30cm/1ft
5 Kniphofia 120cm/4ft
6 Rosemary (evergreen) 120cm/4ft
7 *Artemisia* 'Powis Castle' 90cm/3ft

8 *Choisya ternata* (evergreen) 120cm/4ft
9 Dwarf Michaelmas daisy 60cm/2ft
10 Cistus 45cm/1½ft
11 *Cornus alba* 'Sibirica' 120cm/4ft
12 Existing flagpole cherry (*Prunus* 'Amanogawa') 10m/30ft
13 *Camellia* 'Donation' (evergreen) 200cm/6ft

14 Agapanthus 75cm/2½ ft
15 Hosta 45cm/1½ft
16 Bergenia (evergreen) 30cm/1ft
17 *Anemone* x *hybrida* 75cm/2½ft
18 *Potentilla* 'Princess' 75cm/2½ft
19 Lavender (evergreen) 30cm/1ft
20 *Stachys byzantina* (almost evergreen) 30cm/1ft
21 *Mahonia* 'Charity' (evergreen) 240cm/8ft

WELL-PLANNED GARDENS

Planning a garden involves making informed choices about where to site practical elements such as dustbins (trashcans) and clothes driers as well as more interesting decisions regarding decorative features and plants. This is especially important if your garden is smaller than you would like. Those fortunate enough to have a large back garden sometimes have a small front garden but, as many of these plans show, even an unpromising, tiny, town front garden can be transformed with a little imagination. Many of the ideas and illustrations in this section are, in fact, designed for small gardens but can be adapted easily to larger gardens.

The style of hard landscaping contributes greatly to the success of a garden design, so choose the boundaries and garden floor with care. Make the most of them by erecting a decorative fence, planting a flowering hedge or painting a wall a pale colour to reflect light and to act as a backdrop for wall shrubs and other plants. Choose decorative surfaces such as crazy paving or clay pavers and incorporate interesting textures using gravel beds and feature slabs.

■ ABOVE
A cottage-style front garden bursting with colour and fragrance.

■ OPPOSITE
Clever planting and design of this small town garden has created the
illusion of space.

INSPIRATIONAL IDEAS

When deciding how to design your garden, start with the most prominent features such as dramatic structures or particularly striking plants. Bold statements can be very effective if you only have a small space in which to create an impression.

■ OPPOSITE ABOVE

If a very small garden seems hemmed in by fences, turning the eye inwards towards the centre of the garden can be a good idea. The raised bed becomes the focal point from all parts of this tiny garden, drawing the eye inwards and away from the limitations of the boundary. Sufficient space was left at the end for a small sitting and barbecue area.

■ OPPOSITE BELOW

If you do not have enough time to devote to gardening, then a low-maintenance garden, with as few beds and borders as possible, is ideal. This Japanese-style entrance demonstrates effectively that shape and structure, together with colour, can be more important than the number of plants.

■ BELOW

A moderately sized back garden can have all the elegance of a traditional garden more often associated with grand country houses. It's not only the formal structure of the garden but the strong white-and-silver theme that makes the whole design look well thought out and integrated. Picking up the colour in the paintwork of the gazebo and painting the central plinth white not only echoes the theme but ensures there is relief to the green of the surrounding trees and the box (*Buxus sempervirens*) hedges when the flowers have finished.

INSPIRATIONAL IDEAS

When designing a garden, you should consider the vertical plane. Tall features, like birdbaths, statues and obelisks, can be useful to draw the eye upwards, as can vertical features such as high walls decorated with pots, or trellises clothed with climbers or painted brightly.

■ ABOVE

This narrow plot is typical of many small back gardens, and the straight path to the gate limits the scope without major reconstruction. It benefits greatly from having a gravel path instead of concrete slabs, which would have emphasized the rigidity of the path, and by training the hedge into an arch over the gate. The gate alone would not have been an attractive focal point, but the arch transforms it into an acceptable feature. Having the lawn at the top half of the garden and dense planting at the end, rather than running the lawn along the whole length of the garden, ensures the eye does not take in everything at once. Despite the limitation of size and shape, there is plenty to discover in this garden. The dense planting helps to overcome the lack of structural features.

■ OPPOSITE BELOW

Where space is very sparse, it's a good idea to extend a garden vertically. Although the ground area occupied by this garden is severely limited, the way it has been clothed from ground almost to first floor level has ensured that it is packed with colour and interest. Good use has been made of foliage plants so the display looks well clothed throughout the summer months.

■ ABOVE

Small country cottages and town houses with only a narrow strip of land between house and pavement (footway) or road can cramp the style of even the most enthusiastic garden designer. It may be best to abandon attempts at clever designs and concentrate on a mass of colourful annuals in summer and bulbs in spring. Window boxes and hanging baskets provide additional planting space and give the garden a vertical element, and with such a small garden the regular watering they require should not be an onerous chore.

Painting the wall almost always improves a small garden like this, and helps to show hanging baskets to maximum advantage.

Know-how

BEAUTIFUL BOUNDARIES

There are many ways of decorating the boundaries of a garden. Unattractive walls and fences can be clothed with climbers and wall shrubs or, if the view beyond the garden is an attractive one, it may be worth making a feature of the boundary itself.

■ RIGHT

PICKET FENCES Picket fences are always more attractive than a filled-in panel or closeboard fence. Normally they are left a natural wood colour or painted white, but why not be bold and splash out with the colours? One of these fences has been painted pastel pink to match the roses, the other sugar-almond blue to differentiate between the two properties.

DESIGN TIP *Bear in mind the colours of the flowers in adjoining borders, not only at the time of year when you paint the fence but throughout the rest of the year.*

■ ABOVE

FEATURE FENCE If you get on well with your neighbours, and you want to let in a little light, a fence with "windows" is one solution. Although you may want to modify the style to suit your own taste, the principle of making a feature of your fence is a useful one to bear in mind.

DESIGN TIP *Fences look best if they are maintained at least annually with a fresh coat of preservative or paint. If you want to make a feature of your fence rather than mask it with climbers, be sure to allow for easy access for painting or preserving in your design, not obscuring it with large trees or shrubs.*

■ RIGHT

LIVING FENCE An existing solid fence can be improved by erecting a trellis in front of it and planting climbers such as clematis and roses. Here, a figure has been sited to bring a sense of summer enchantment, and also to provide a focal point in winter when the foliage cover has gone.

DESIGN TIP *If you find an exposed trellis unattractive in winter, include an evergreen such as ivy. But bear in mind that evergreens that twine through their support make maintenance of the trellis and fence difficult.*

■ BELOW

CAVITY WALLS Low walls are often better than tall ones for a small front garden, but plain single-skin walls can look drab and uninspiring. Building one with a cavity like this not only provides more planting space but also helps to bridge and link both sides of the garden boundary.

DESIGN TIP *Unless the boundary has to deter animals, a low wall or even a small-post-and-chain-link fence is effective. It is also possible to mark the boundary by planting up to the edge of a bed, which can be viewed from both sides.*

Know-how
INTEGRATING THE PRACTICALITIES

Planning should also involve practical essentials like somewhere to dry the washing and a hide for the dustbin (trashcan), as well as more stimulating features like a built-in barbecue. The most attractive garden can become an irritation if there's nowhere to dry the clothes or there's an inconvenient walk to put out the household refuse.

■ LEFT
CLOTHES DRIER The only space for a clothes drier in this small garden was in the paved area shown. A rotary drier was chosen with the socket well hidden by beach pebbles where one of the paving slabs had been removed. This makes it possible to remove the drier when it is not in use, leaving the garden relatively unaffected by this necessity.

DESIGN TIP *Try to avoid a clothes line that runs straight down the garden, or across it at a conspicuous spot. Unless removed after use each time, it will visually divide the garden. Rotary driers can sometimes be masked completely by screen block walling in a convenient corner.*

■ LEFT
BARBECUES Even
if your use of the
barbecue is infrequent,
having one built in
gives the impression of
a garden well thought
out and cleverly
designed. All the racks
and basic equipment
can be bought as kits,
so usually you only
have to build the walls.
DESIGN TIP *Obtain
specifications from kit
manufacturers at the
design stage. Armed with
the dimensions
of your preferred kit, it
will be easier to integrate
it into the brickwork or
ensure that it's a good fit
with the particular
walling block that you
are planning to use.*

■ LEFT
DRAINS Drain inspection covers
sound mundane, but they are important
where they occur in the middle of a
crucial part of the garden, such as a patio
or in the lawn. These metal covers
immediately attract the eye, rather like
an unattractive focal point, detracting
from the more desirable elements.

Special replacement covers that have a
planting cavity or a shallow tray to hold
paving are available. It is important to
cut the paving accurately to ensure a
neat appearance.
DESIGN TIP *Don't place a container
over an inspection cover: it will only draw
attention to the cover, which will probably
project beneath the base of the container.*

■ RIGHT
REFUSE This corner of a small garden
can double as a built-in patio, barbecue
or a refuse hide, depending on what's
most applicable.
DESIGN TIP *Keep as many utilities as
possible together in a small area if possible.
This will minimize their impact on the rest
of the garden.*

Know-how
CREATING ILLUSIONS

Illusions are useful design devices, whatever the size of garden, but they are especially valuable in small ones. Mostly they are used to suggest that the garden is larger or more densely planted than it is in reality.

■ ABOVE

BEYOND THE DOOR Doors and gates suggest that it's possible to explore more of the garden. This large gate is clearly part of a garden on a grand scale, but you might be able to come to an arrangement with a neighbour to set a decorative gate between your two properties. If you are on friendly terms you can actually use it, otherwise agree to keep it locked. Both will benefit from the impression that the garden extends beyond its real limits.
DESIGN TIP *If using this kind of device, it's best if both gardens have a path leading to the gate, so that it really does look as though there's more garden to explore.*

■ LEFT

PAINTED ILLUSIONS If you are artistically talented, or can draw upon the services of someone who is, painting a false perspective into a scene that suggests a path or border continues can be surprisingly convincing. Here the path turns to the left immediately beyond the gate, but at first glance it appears as though it continues beyond.
DESIGN TIP *This kind of design device works most convincingly where the scene appears to continue beyond a door or gate.*

■ LEFT

ENDLESS PATHS Dense planting with tall shrubs or trees at the end of a garden can suggest that the property goes further, even though the path turns or leads nowhere in particular. The effect works best in summer, when plants are in full leaf.

DESIGN TIP *A path will give the illusion of being longer if it tapers towards the far end. Dense planting at the perimeter of the garden also helps to imply there's more garden beyond.*

■ BELOW

DECEPTIVE TRELLIS Decorative trellis is usually more pleasing than a plain wall, and hints at things beyond.
DESIGN TIP *If using trellis ornamentally, do not over-plant and avoid covering it with climbers.*

Know-how
USING VERTICALS

You may be fortunate enough to have a garden in which the verticals are supplied by mature trees, but it is more usual for the boundaries and house walls to provide this vertical element. Arches, pergolas and trellises are useful for adding height within the garden, especially before newly planted small trees can play a role, and much can be achieved by covering existing walls and fences with climbers and wall shrubs.

■ LEFT
BUILT-UP BORDERS A small town or courtyard garden can appear almost claustrophobic, but it's possible to make a virtue of its enclosed nature by surrounding yourself with lush growth. Build up the borders all around to create a secret hideaway.
DESIGN TIP
This kind of planting works best if the borders have irregular outlines extending towards the centre, rather than straight, narrow borders. Use tubs to draw the eye into the centre. Use plenty of evergreens and variegated plants, and medium-sized with small plants towards the front of the border and climbers and tall plants at the back.

■ OPPOSITE ABOVE

STYLISH SUPPORTS Climbing and rambling roses require a suitable support, and although wires can be stretched at intervals along the wall, a trellis is more decorative. This is especially useful if the wall itself is not particularly attractive as the trellis remains a feature even when the rose is bare.

DESIGN TIP *Try extending the trellis beyond the height of the wall or fence. This will produce a better display of roses and also ensure fewer thorny stems hanging where they could be a hazard.*

■ RIGHT

AVENUE OF ARCHES As most of the height was provided by the boundary and house walls, with a void in the centre, an ornate avenue of arches has been used to take the eye to the centre of the garden. It also creates a corridor linking two distinct areas of the garden. When the climbers have covered the frame, the tunnel effect will be emphasized.

DESIGN TIP *If the garden is small, it may be best to angle a pergola or arch to take the eye at an angle. This prevents the whole garden being absorbed at a glance.*

■ ABOVE

CLIMBERS AS CLOTHING Clothe the house wall whenever possible. Although the temptation is to use evergreens such as ivies, if the property is attractive in its own right, make use of seasonal flowering climbers such as roses and wisterias.

DESIGN TIP *Deciduous climbers such as roses are shown to advantage against a painted wall. Only those plants that can be lowered easily from the wall for periodic painting of the house are practical choices, however.*

■ ABOVE

COVERED IN CLIMBERS Clothing the lower level of a house will make the most of vertical space in a tiny garden. Here a colourful, evergreen *Euonymus fortunei* variety has been used beneath the window, and pyracanthas for greater height either side.

DESIGN TIP *Evergreens are a good choice for this kind of position, but use bright flowers near the base to pack a punch and give the garden colour.*

Planning and Planting
BEATIFUL BASEMENT

A basement garden can be transformed into a delightful
outdoor room like this, with planning and clever planting.
One advantage of an enclosed space is the low cost: the
expense is limited by the amount you can pack in.

PLANNING

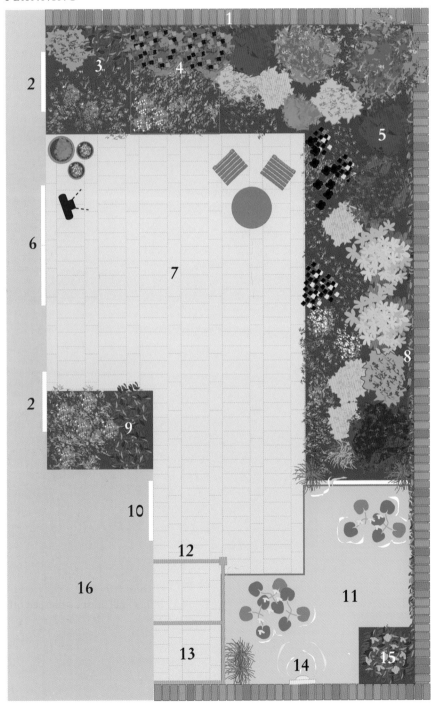

KEY TO PLAN

1 Wall
2 Window
3 Ground-level bed with
   mixed planting
4 Low-level raised bed with
   mixed planting
5 High-level raised bed with
   mixed planting
6 French window or patio
   door
7 Patio paved with slabs
8 Climbers on wall
9 Dwarf shrubs
10 Back door
11 Pond
12 Pergola
13 Space for dustbin
   (trashcan)
14 Wall fountain
15 Small bed with specimen
   shrub
16 House

🔦 Viewpoint on photograph

Basement gardens often seem
unpromising at first – dark and
uninteresting with little to bring
cheer or admiration. But if you
paint the walls white to reflect as
much light as possible, add some
raised beds to provide more
impressive planting areas, install a
pond with wall fountain, and buy
some stylish garden furniture, then
you have a garden packed with
interest and impact.

In a basement garden like this,
accommodating practicalities such
as the dustbin (trashcan) is always
a problem. The best solution is to
tuck the unsightly necessities
away at the back where they will
not be visible from seating areas.
Washing lines can be replaced with
a rotary drier, which can be stored
when not in use. Dustbins can be
tucked away in the alcove formed
by the pergola.

PLANTING

RAISED BEDS

Bricks are a better choice than walling blocks for raised beds built close to the house. Even if a different kind of brick is used, it is likely to blend more harmoniously with the building than concrete or reconstituted stone blocks.

Bricklaying low walls is not a difficult skill to acquire, and the wall will go up surprisingly quickly once the footing has been prepared. You can always hire a professional if you don't have the time to build a wall yourself.

HOW TO BUILD A RAISED BED

1 All walls require a footing. For a low wall, the thickness of a single row of bricks is required. A double row of bricks is required for a taller wall. Excavate a trench about 30cm (1ft) deep, and place about 13cm (5in) of consolidated hardcore in the bottom. Drive pegs in so the tops are at the final height of the base. Use a spirit level to check levels.

2 Fill with a concrete mix of 1 part cement, 2 parts sharp sand, and 3 parts aggregate, and level it off with the peg tops. After the concrete has hardened (1–2 days) lay the bricks on a bed of mortar. Place a wedge of mortar at one end of each brick to be laid. For stability, make a pier at each end, and at intervals of 1.8–2.4m (6–8ft) if the wall is long.

3 For subsequent courses, lay a ribbon or mortar on top of the previous row, then "butter" one end of the brick to be laid. Tap level, checking constantly with a spirit level. The wall must be finished off with a coping of suitable bricks or with special coping sold for the purpose.

Planning and Planting
A PRIVATE GARDEN

Privacy is an important part of a well-planned garden, especially if it is overlooked by other properties. If you want seclusion, plant plenty of tall evergreens around the perimeter. Most of the design elements are then thrown towards the centre of the garden, so that the eye is taken inwards and the garden does not seem claustrophobic.

KEY TO PLAN

1	Conifer	8	Seasonal plants
2	Specimen evergreen shrub	9	Plants in pots
		10	Patio
3	Ground cover	11	Seating area
4	Evergreen shrub	12	Crazy-paved patio
5	Gravel		
6	Planted container and ornaments	13	House
		⚒	Viewpoint on photograph
7	Feature slab		

This garden looks in on itself, with all the colour and bright plants running along the centre of the garden. The dense evergreen planting around the boundary and the use of conifers and other tall evergreens ensure a feeling of seclusion and privacy.

It is important to avoid a ribbon effect when a main path runs the length of the garden, so the path here has been broken up with decorative feature slabs, and patches of gravel take the eye outwards to the flowerbeds on either side. By mixing paving materials and taking the path out to the sides in an irregular manner, the eye is drawn to the planted areas and not just along the path.

TUBS AND POTS
The larger the pot or container, the more plants you can pack in and the more they are likely to thrive in the generous amount of potting soil.

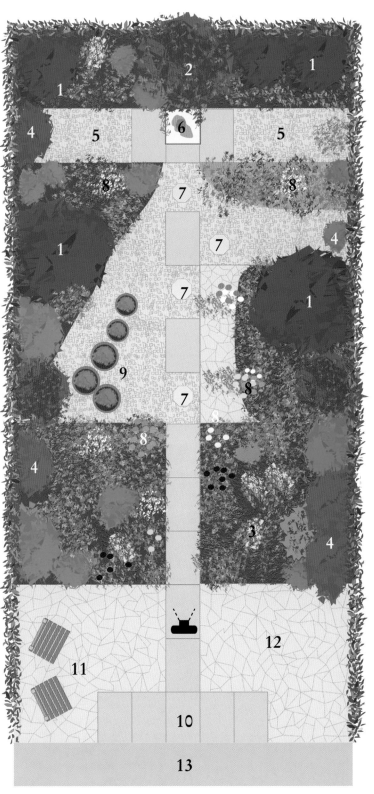

PLANTING TUBS AND PATIO POTS

1 Filled tubs and pots can be heavy to move, so plant them up in their final positions if possible. Cover the drainage holes with a layer of broken pots, large gravel or chipped bark.

2 A loam-based potting mixture is best for most plants, but if the pot is to be used where weight is a consideration, such as on a balcony, use a peat-based or peat-substitute mixture.

3 Choose a tall or bold plant for the centre, such as *Cordyline australis* or a fuchsia, or one with large flowers such as the osteospermum that has been used here.

PLANTING

4 Fill in around the base with some bushier but lower-growing plants. Choose bright flowers if the centrepiece is a foliage plant, but place the emphasis on foliage effect if the focal point is a flowering plant.

5 Cover the surface with a decorative mulch such as chipped bark or cocoa shells if much of the surface is visible (this is worth doing anyway to conserve moisture). Water thoroughly.

Planning and Planting
WAYS WITH WALLS

The perimeter walls of some gardens can be oppressive, yet masking them with evergreen plants may emphasize the gloominess. This design opens up the centre and uses decorative trellis to make a feature of the walls.

PLANNING

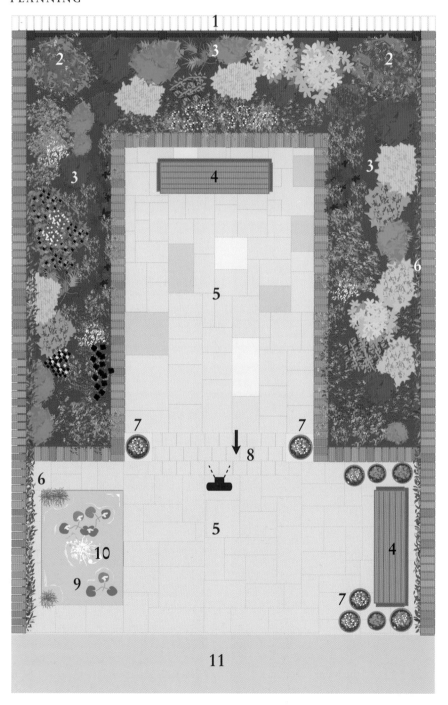

Decorative trellises ensure instant impact and will in time be covered with plants, preventing walls looking dull or oppressive. A white trellis looks good against a green backdrop of foliage, but don't be afraid to use a dark colour against a wall, especially if the wall is white or a light colour.

The raised beds in this design elevate the plants, so the boundary walls behind do not appear quite so high. Similarly, a change of level adds interest, but to relieve the possible dominance of the paving in the lower area a formal pond complete with fountain provides a focal point, especially when viewed from the garden seat on the opposite side.

WATER LILIES
Plant water lilies in spring, before the leaves have fully expanded. They can be planted in special planting baskets or in a container with solid sides, such as an old washing-up bowl.

PLANTING

HOW TO PLANT A WATER LILY

1 Use a heavy soil that is not too rich in nutrients. Aquatic planting soil is available from aquatic specialists.

2 Don't add ordinary fertilizers to the soil, as they may cause a proliferation of algae. Use a slow-release fertilizer.

3 Remove the water lily from its container, and plant it in the new container at its original depth.

4 Add a layer of gravel to reduce the chance of fish disturbing the soil. It also helps to keep the soil in place when the container is lowered into the water.

5 Flood the container with water and let it stand for a while. This reduces the chance of the water becoming muddy when you lower it into the pond.

6 Place the container in a shallow part of the pond initially, especially if new leaves are about to develop. Move it into deeper water a week or two later.

Planning and Planting
URBAN ELEGANCE

This town garden is the perfect place to relax in, to unwind from the stresses of a busy life. The dominance of greens and whites in the planting plan gives the garden a sense of unity and subtlety, as well as a sense of cool tranquillity.

PLANNING

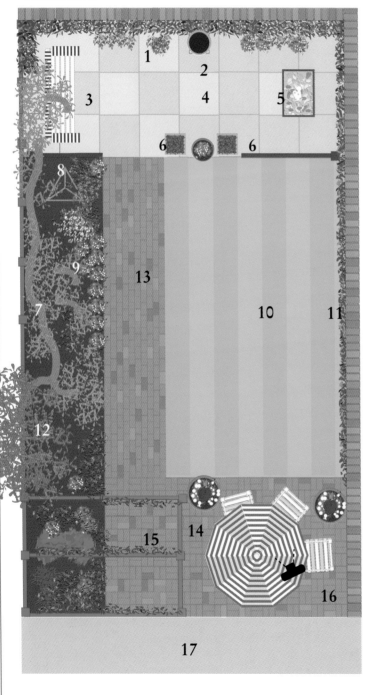

KEY TO PLAN

1 Hedge
2 Urn
3 Garden swing seat
4 Paved area
5 Pebble fountain
6 Clipped box
7 Trellis
8 Tripod for climbers
9 Low raised bed with mixed planting
10 Lawn
11 Wall climbers
12 Specimen tree, pruned and trained to grow along boundary
13 Brick path
14 Patio overhead (beams above window level)
15 Climber over patio overhead
16 Patio
17 House
🔨 Viewpoint on photograph

This is primarily the kind of garden that would appeal to adults, but there is a large lawn for anyone who needs to let off steam. However, a high-quality lawn like this is too good for rough play: a paved area is more suitable for ball games or frequent use. The lawn is an important and dominant design feature of this plan, creating a sense of open space that lets the garden "breathe".

The tree on the left-hand side of the garden is unusual as it has been persuaded to grow along the edge of the garden rather than over it, so avoiding a potential shade problem. A small tree, left to grow naturally, would be just as effective in this situation.

As planting space is limited, the bed along the side of the garden accommodates seasonal plants and permanent evergreen plants, to pack in colour where it's needed, and to introduce an element of variety from season to season.

■ RIGHT

HOW TO BUILD PATIO OVERHEADS

Patio overheads are a kind of pergola with one end of the overhead beams fixed to the house or garden wall. These are particularly effective for linking the home and garden visually, and of course they provide a useful support for climbers as well as a degree of shade. If you want a more enclosed structure, with permanent shading and a greater degree of privacy, it's possible to fix reed mats over the top, although

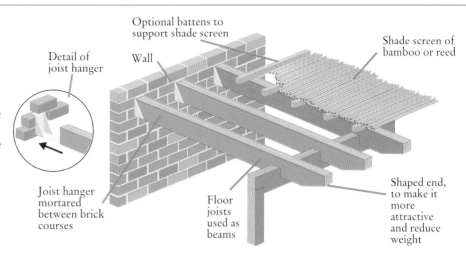

Detail of joist hanger

Optional battens to support shade screen

Wall

Shade screen of bamboo or reed

Joist hanger mortared between brick courses

Floor joists used as beams

Shaped end, to make it more attractive and reduce weight

PLANNING

additional battens, laid at right angles to the overhead beams, will be required to support them.

Remember that patio overheads that join the house should always be high enough to clear the window and not block out the view if vigorous climbers cascade from the beams.

Use floor joists for the overhead beams, and secure them to the wall with joist hangers (see illustration). These are designed with a lip to be mortared into the brickwork, so on an existing wall it will be necessary to chisel out sufficient mortar to accommodate the hanger. Once the joist hanger has been mortared into position and the mortar has set, the beam can be inserted and secured by nailing through the fixing holes in the hanger. The hangers are available from builders' merchants and large do-it-yourself stores.

If the span is short, the beams may only require the support of one cross-beam supported on posts, as shown. Wider spans will need intermediate post and beam supports.

If you wish to add shading for summer, nail battens parallel to the wall to support a reed or bamboo screen (these usually come in rolls), as shown in the illustration. If you wish to have the shading in position only for the summer, it should be possible to tie it in position, but do this securely.

Be sure that the posts are strong enough for the structure and that they are well concreted into the ground or fixed in special post supports.

Planning and Planting
SIMPLE SHAPES

Simple garden designs using geometric shapes that are obvious and easy to see can be very effective. They ensure that the garden looks uncluttered. In this garden it is the choice of plants that will transform it from a simple plan to a striking and well-designed garden with plenty of impact. The design pivots around a diamond-shaped lawn, set on the angle of the brick pathway.

PLANNING

KEY TO PLAN

1 Metal fence
2 Gate
3 Specimen shrub
4 Dwarf shrubs and evergreen border plants
5 Path of clay pavers with "rope" edging
6 Corsican mint (*Mentha requienii*) lawn edged with brick
7 Bay window
8 House

🎥 Viewpoint on photograph

Dividing a garden with a straight path from door to gate is not very imaginative, and has the added effect of slicing it into two smaller pieces. Don't be afraid to keep the design simple, though. Here, by positioning the gate towards the centre of the boundary it has been possible to introduce a strong line, while varying the depths of the beds allows for more interesting planting. Even so, this arrangement could have still been dull without the extra dimension created by the Corsican mint lawn. This can be used as an intimate sitting area, but its role as a textural feature is equally important.

In the photograph opposite, the plants are still small; after a season or two little of the soil or mulch would be visible.

CHOOSING A NON-GRASS LAWN
Corsican mint and thyme lawns can be planted in the same way – in the photographs opposite, thyme is being used.

PLANTING

HOW TO PLANT NON-LAWN GRASS

1 Thoroughly dig over the area and clear the ground of weeds at least a month before planting. Hoe off any seedlings that appear in the meantime. Rake the ground level before planting.

2 Water the plants in their pots, then set them out about 15–20cm (6–8in) apart, in staggered rows to work out the position and how many plants you need.

3 Knock a plant from its pot and carefully tease out a few of the roots if they are running tightly around the edge of the pot.

4 Plant to the original depth, and firm the soil around the roots before knocking out and planting the next plant. Water thoroughly and keep well watered for the first season.

Planning and Planting
CREATING FOCAL POINTS

Focal points like the chimney pot and container in this plan are an asset in any garden. They take the eye to individual elements within the design rather than letting it pass straight over the garden from gate to door in a single glance. No well-planned garden should be without such finishing touches.

PLANNING

reflect the style associated with the period in which the house was built. In a garden like this, where the house forms a dominant backdrop, it's important that home and garden look well integrated and harmonize as much as possible.

A NEAT EDGE
Emphasize the profile of your beds and borders, as well as your paths, by giving them a crisp or interesting edge. Select an edging that suits the style of your garden. If you prefer an old-fashioned look, reproduction edgings are now readily available.

OTHER IDEAS

Try using empty wine bottles, neck-down, for an unusual edging – leave just a couple of centimetres (an inch) or so of bottle showing.

If you live in a coastal area, consider using large seashells for an edging.

Here containers of various kinds have been used as focal points, and they are especially useful at those times of the year when there is little colour and plants in the borders have died back. Like the previous design, the path has a diversion, which avoids a straight walk from gate to door.

Although modern paving setts have been used for the path, a "rope" edging has been used to

PLANTING

NEAT EDGING

1 For a period garden, Victorian-style rope edging looks appropriate. You can use it to retain a gravel path or as an edging to a paved path.

2 Wavy-edged edgings like this are also reminiscent of some of the older styles of garden, but they can also be used to advantage in a modern setting to give a formal effect.

3 Sawn log rolls make a strong and attractive edging where you want a flowerbed to be raised slightly above a lawn, but remember it may be difficult to mow right up to the edge.

Planning and Planting
NEAT CORNERING

Corner sites can present special problems, but this design has unusually managed to marry straight lines and curves in a successful and distinctive way. It sometimes pays to be bold and imaginative when the site is a difficult one.

PLANNING

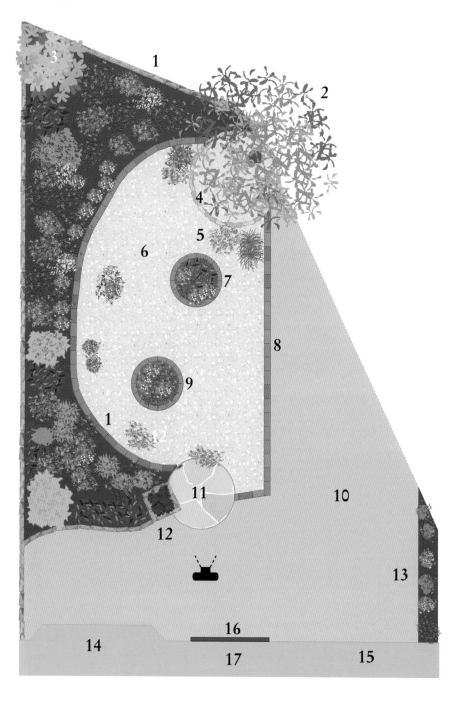

KEY TO PLAN

1 Low wall
2 Birch tree
3 Mixed planting
4 Raised circular bed
5 Plants in gravel
6 Gravel
7 Brick-edged bed with perennials
8 Brick edge
9 Brick-edged bed with seasonal plants
10 Drive
11 Circular stone area
12 Stone pillar with planting area
13 Dwarf shrubs
14 Bay window
15 Garage
16 Door
17 House

⬛ Viewpoint on photograph

Awkward corner sites can be especially difficult to design, and if they also have to accommodate a driveway too, the problem is further compounded.

Maximum use has been made of the existing birch tree in this plan, as it takes the eye from the bleakness of the drive. Creating a circular bed around it emphasizes it as a focal point, and to give the garden a sense of unity, the circular theme has been repeated with a couple of round raised beds and an interesting circular stone feature, linking the drive and gravel area.

USING GRAVEL
Gravel is best laid over a weed-suppressing base, but it's still possible to plant through both materials if necessary.

PLANTING

HOW TO LAY AND PLANT THROUGH GRAVEL

1 Dig the area to hold 5cm (2in) of gravel. Level the ground, then lay heavy-duty black plastic or a mulching sheet over the area. Overlap strips by about 5cm (2in).

2 Tip gravel on to the sheet, then rake it level. To plant through the gravel, draw back an area of gravel from where you plan to plant and make a slit in the plastic.

3 Plant normally through the slit, enriching the soil beneath if necessary with fertilizer or garden compost.

4 Firm in the plant with your hand and water thoroughly, then smooth the plastic back and re-cover the area with gravel.

Choosing Plants

PLANTS FOR SMALL GARDENS

Almost any plant other than medium-sized or tall trees or very large shrubs and rampant ground cover can be grown in a small garden. Often quite large plants are used, but they need to be pruned back regularly to maintain a compact size. Whenever possible, it's best to choose naturally compact plants that won't become a nuisance.

EVERGREEN TREES

If conifers are excluded, there are few evergreen trees suitable for a small garden. Few broad-leaved trees are evergreen in temperate climates, and unfortunately many of those that are, such as the evergreen oak (*Quercus ilex*), grow far too large for most gardens. There are some worth searching out, such as *Drimys winteri*, which is too large for a tiny garden, but is not a fast grower. It's not a good choice for cold areas, however. Hollies (ilex) are really tough, and can be trained into a conical or standard tree with a clear trunk.

Drimys winteri is an uncommon plant, especially where winters are cold, but it makes an interesting large shrub or small tree with large, leathery evergreen leaves and fragrant white flowers in late spring.

DECIDUOUS TREES

It's a pity to exclude trees from a small garden, but choose those that remain small and have more than one season of interest. *Acer griseum*, for example, has a lovely cinnamon bark which looks

Crataegus oxyacantha (now more correctly *C. laevigata*) 'Rosea Flore Pleno' is a pretty hawthorn with double pink flowers in late spring. These trees never become very large.

wonderful in winter sunlight as well as fantastic in autumn colour. Many hawthorns (crataegus) make pleasing compact trees for a small garden. For flowering trees, look for those with columnar growth, such as *Prunus* 'Amanogawa'.

CONIFERS

Conifers come in many shades of gold and green (some with a hint of blue), as well as various shapes and sizes. The vast majority are evergreen. Unfortunately, most of them grow far too tall for a small garden. Select those with narrow, columnar growth that will not ultimately become too tall. Some to look for are *Juniperus scopulorum* 'Skyrocket', *Juniperus communis* 'Hibernica' and *Taxus baccata* 'Fastigiata Aurea'. *Cupressus macrocarpa* 'Goldcrest' also has a pleasing upright profile as well as a bright colour.

DWARF CONIFERS

A visit to any garden centre will reveal a bewildering choice of dwarf conifers, but always check on likely size after say 10 or 15 years of growth. Some will remain dwarf and may even be at home in

Cupressus macrocarpa 'Goldcrest' eventually makes a medium-sized tree, but has a narrow growth that means it does not take up excessive ground space. Young foliage is a beautiful yellow.

a rock garden; others may grow surprisingly large. Among those that grow shrub-size are *Thuja orientalis* 'Aurea Nana', *Thuja occidentalis* 'Rheingold' and *Chamaecyparis pisifera* 'Filifera Aurea'. *Juniperus squamata* 'Blue Star' remains low-growing, and there are many other ground-hugging conifers.

EVERGREEN SHRUBS

You will be spoilt for choice with evergreen shrubs, so decide how large or small you want the plant

Thuja occidentalis 'Rheingold' is slow-growing and forms an oval to conical bush that always looks neat. The colour is old gold, and is especially pleasing in winter.

to grow to reduce your short list. If you have an acid soil, rhododendrons are a likely choice, but some can grow huge while others are suitable for a rock garden. There are bound to be varieties of appropriate size for your needs. Hebes are also available in many shapes and sizes, but always check that the ones you like are winter-hardy in your area. Heathers are evergreen and they are bound to be compact enough for your garden. The winter-flowering *Erica carnea* varieties are especially useful.

Hebe x *franciscana* 'Variegata' is a delightfully bright and compact dwarf shrub, but it may suffer – or even be killed – where winters are cold.

DECIDUOUS SHRUBS

The problem with many deciduous shrubs is their short period of interest: flowering sometimes lasting no more than a couple of weeks. To make the best use of space, choose some that have golden or variegated foliage for a longer period of interest, or select those that have early colour, like chaenomeles, which bloom in spring, or that have late-season interest, like *Cotoneaster horizontalis* with its bright berries and vivid autumn foliage colour. Some, such as hydrangeas, also retain their flowers for a long period, and the dead heads also make an interesting winter feature.

The flower colour of *Hydrangea macrophylla* is often affected by the acidity or alkalinity of the soil.

BORDER PLANTS

All but the largest and tallest or most rampant herbaceous plants are suitable for a small garden, but where space is limited it's best to concentrate on those that flower early or late, or that look good over a long period and don't only look good for a week or two in summer. Lupins look fantastic for a couple of weeks, but for the rest of the season offer little interest.

Doronicums have nothing to offer by the time summer arrives, but they make an eye-catching display in spring.

Select summer flowers that bloom over a long period, or that have attractive foliage. For early border flowers, doronicums, with their yellow daisy-type flowers, look good, while at the end of the season schizostylis and varieties and hybrids of *Sedum spectabile* will sustain the colour.

EVERGREEN BORDER PLANTS

Make a point of visiting gardens in winter, and note which border plants remain evergreen. There are not many of them, but they are invaluable for sustaining interest during the bleak months. They include bergenias, ajugas and *Stachys byzantina*.

Ajuga reptans 'Atropurpurea' is one of several attractive bugles that make an attractive edging. They are almost evergreen and grow in sun and shade.

PATIOS, BALCONIES AND ROOF GARDENS

No garden should be designed without a place to sit, and, although garden benches and attractive seats tucked away in an arbour or alcove are always inviting, it's worth including a patio or an area where a group can sit and relax together, and perhaps enjoy a light meal or a drink surrounded by the sights and sounds of the garden.

If your garden is very small, or virtually non-existent, a patio or even a balcony may serve as the garden, in which case it is your extra room, the room outside. Where there's space, patios offer plenty of design scope.

It's natural to place a patio near the house, which is practical if you use the patio for meals, but it doesn't have to be a rectangle placed directly outside the patio doors. You could angle the patio around the corner of the house. It doesn't even have to be close to the dwelling – the design may be more impressive if the patio is at the end of the garden, or even to one side.

■ ABOVE
A shady retreat for dining al fresco, combining natural wooden benches
with a sturdy stone table.

■ OPPOSITE
Where space is at a premium, a small curved bench can provide an attractive
sitting area. Position it where you can enjoy the fruits of your labours.

INSPIRATIONAL IDEAS

You should consider carefully whether you want a patio filled with plants and flowers or something more structural or "architectural", with few plants and a big impact. A successful patio is often an extension of the style of the house.

■ LEFT
Balcony gardens can be striking in their simplicity. This one is large and has the benefit of a solid wall, which offers privacy as well as shelter from wind. A similar style could be used for a patio if you have plenty of space in the rest of the garden to indulge your taste in plants. This design shows strikingly the effect of form and shape, and the design value of "void", an area left uncluttered by garden furniture or tall plants.

■ OPPOSITE

A contemporary garden for a warm climate. Tall cacti grow out of the gravel, and rocks and stones are positioned among the beds to add interest. This truly is a garden for relaxing and enjoying the sun. The black furniture suits the modern, minimalist style of the garden.

■ ABOVE

The style of this sitting area could not be a greater contrast to the white-walled balcony shown opposite, top. Here, the garden is wrapped around the seating, a kind of mini-patio tucked away within the main planting areas. This is not the kind of area suitable for entertaining or for the family to relax together, but is a cosier, more intimate, place where a couple can rendezvous, or two or three friends can relax to discuss the pleasures of gardening.

INSPIRATIONAL IDEAS

If gardening on a balcony, in limited space, you'll want to cram in as many plants as possible, but in a large garden with plenty of flowerbeds you may prefer not to be bothered by bees and insects attracted by flowers while you are relaxing or eating.

■ LEFT
A secluded sitting area surrounded by plants has a special appeal. It becomes part of the garden proper rather than an isolated patio. White-painted furniture helps to make a statement in an area that could otherwise become cluttered visually. The white-painted trellis also helps to make a visual boundary and creates the impression of a more designed and integrated area by picking up the colour theme from the white garden furniture.

■ ABOVE

In a large garden, an area like this makes an ideal, sheltered retreat. The overhead beams not only create the illusion of an outdoor room but also provide support for a variety of evergreen climbers. Although climbers provide a wonderful natural canopy, bear in mind that the support must be high enough for trailing shoots not to become a nuisance below. This is especially important if climbing roses are planted, as the thorns are a potential hazard.

■ RIGHT

Balconies can be exposed to the elements, and sitting on a balcony can be a public experience. Using plenty of plants, including climbers, helps to overcome these problems, and from a gardening viewpoint transforms a barren area of paving into a haven of beauty. Here, vertical curtains of green have been achieved by planting climbers and wall shrubs against the dwelling wall, and by fixing a climbing frame to the edge of the balcony.

Know-how

SOMEWHERE TO SIT

Gardens should be places to relax in as well as to work in, and although a deckchair or lounger on the lawn is a good way to while away a few sunny hours, a patio or balcony garden room should be designed for relaxation and recreation, planned and furnished to become an enticing place to eat or drink al fresco.

No patio or balcony garden is complete without somewhere to sit, and the style and materials of the garden furniture used can have a profound effect on how the feature is perceived. No matter how cleverly designed and well constructed the patio, an inappropriate table and chairs can spoil the effect, while well-chosen seats and tables can make even a mediocre patio look good.

■ ABOVE
FOLD-AWAY CHAIRS Balconies pose a special problem as space is usually limited. Rather than normal garden chairs, consider directors' chairs, which can be folded to take indoors.
DESIGN TIP *Design a balcony garden so that there is good access and an area where several people can gather to sit together without fear of falling over plants or pots. This may mean grouping containers together into a few choice areas, but the impact will not be diminished.*

■ OPPOSITE LOWER LEFT
ALUMINIUM Cast aluminium alloy furniture has the appeal of the old cast-iron types that it replicates, with the huge advantage of light weight. This type of garden furniture is available in a range of colours.
DESIGN TIP *Greens and browns will blend into the garden, whereas white will stand out. Choose a colour that reflects the effect you want to create.*

■ LEFT
WOOD Informal wooden garden furniture like this blends in beautifully. Here, the seat is arranged much as it might be in an indoor room, which helps to give it the impression of being an extension of the home.
DESIGN TIP *Position your furniture to take advantage of the garden's colours, scents and view. A fragrant climber will add to your enjoyment of the garden as you survey your handiwork.*

■ BELOW

BENCH SEATS Bench tables with integrated seats can be reminiscent of public picnic places, but small stylish ones will banish any suggestion of lack of taste. This one has been varnished to keep its natural appeal, which makes it attractive as well as practical.

DESIGN TIP *Avoid placing a rectangular table at right angles to the wall or edge of the paving. It will probably look more pleasing if angled, like the one illustrated.*

■ ABOVE

NATURAL MATERIALS Cane and wicker furniture is not ideal for leaving out in poor weather, but it is usually light enough to be carried under cover. It is also a good choice for a balcony. This type of chair adds to the impression that your patio or balcony is just an extension of the home.

DESIGN TIP *White furniture stands out well from a background of plants. However, in a bright, sunny place with lots of paving and few plants, white can look stark. Choose a colour that's appropriate to the setting.*

MATERIAL MATTERS

Patio furniture varies widely in price and quality, and there should be something to suit every taste and pocket. The starting point, however, should be what looks right rather than a prejudice about a particular material or concern over price. It may be better to buy one really good piece of furniture rather than several cheaper pieces, but sometimes inexpensive furniture is perfectly adequate for a particular situation.

Plastics and resins are often dismissed, but some types make strong furniture that lasts well and is easy to wipe clean, stack and store. If those qualities, especially portability, are important, don't dismiss these materials.

Timber furniture is always a popular choice, but here you probably do pay for quality. Hardwood furniture that is well made to last for years is not cheap, and it can be heavy to move around. It will also require annual cleaning and treating with a suitable oil or preservative if its colour is to remain strong and bright.

Cast-iron garden furniture is still available, and looks right where a period atmosphere is being created, but it's extremely heavy to move. Cast-aluminium alloy imitations look as good yet are light and easy to move. They are worth the extra cost.

Aluminium alloy furniture is usually painted or coated in a special resin. White is a popular colour, but it shows dirt easily. Browns, greens, even blues, are colours that do not show the dirt so readily, and look stylish too.

Know-how
A SUITABLE POSITION

Be imaginative about where you position the sitting and outdoor dining area – it doesn't necessarily have to adjoin the house, and it doesn't have to be a conventional patio shape. There are many other options, and the possibilities are limited only by imagination.

■ RIGHT
CLOSE FOR COMFORT There's much to be said in favour of a patio close to the house – especially if you do plenty of entertaining. It is also convenient for watering containers from the kitchen tap, and handy for harvesting culinary herbs planted in containers.
DESIGN TIP *Angling a patio at 45 degrees to the building makes it that little bit more distinctive and takes full advantage of the sun as it moves around.*

■ BELOW
A SHELTERED SPOT This is a
traditional patio, in a sheltered position
close to the house. It is purely functional,
but for many gardeners that's what's
required, and in this country cottage
setting it blends in with the rest of the
garden. The slight change of level

between paving and lawn helps to
delineate the patio area.
DESIGN TIP *Choose a position that's
sheltered from too much sun or rain, and
not exposed to cold winds. Shade for part
of the day is not a drawback, and is often
welcome, but make sure that the patio
receives sun for at least part of the day.*

■ ABOVE
THE CENTRE OF ATTENTION
Few would think of a sitting area in the
centre of the garden, but it gives the
impression of a garden designed for,
and built around, people. Tasteful
garden furniture is essential in this
position, as it will become part of the
main focal point of the garden.
DESIGN TIP *Don't be afraid to be
different. It may bring that special quality
to your garden that makes it personal,
individual and powerful in a design sense.*

■ OPPOSITE
A PERMANENT OASIS This
distinctive feature packs all the punch
you could wish for. It's been sited away
from the house, where the garden can
be viewed in its full spendour, and is
positioned to take advantage of the sun
during the afternoon. Its position in the
centre of the lawn acts as one of the
focal points of the garden. The
lightweight seating is easy to move
around when required, while the fixed
table, with its special planting area in
the centre, looks good at all times.
DESIGN TIP *Don't be afraid to make
your garden look lived in, or to be daring
when it comes to built-in furniture! It can
be a gamble that pays off.*

OBSERVATION PAYS

It's important to get the patio
position right, and what appears
to be a good position when
planned on paper may have
serious shortcomings in reality. It
pays to sit out in the garden a few
times, on different days, and
ideally at different times of year,
to assess whether it's a
comfortable position as well as
one that works in design terms.
   You will soon discover whether
shade, drips from trees or chilling
winds caused by a wind-funnel

effect between buildings are likely
to be a problem. It will also give a
better idea of privacy – if you
don't want to be overlooked, it
may be necessary to erect a screen
or reposition the patio. A wall or
a hedge might provide a private or
sheltered position, or a patio
overhead of beams supported on
posts may give a sufficient degree
of privacy. These can all be
worked into the design and
should be incorporated at the
planning stage.

Know-how
EATING OUT

A meal outdoors always seems to taste better than the same food served at the dining-room table. A barbecue may be a bit smoky from time to time, and there may be the odd wasp to contend with, but it's all so much more fun. It isn't necessary to design your patio with meals in mind, but if you plan to do a lot of eating out it makes sense to consider the practicalities.

PORTABLE BARBECUES

Built-in barbecues look stylish
and give the impression of a
well-planned garden, but where
space is limited, they may not
be the best solution. Portable
barbecues that can be wheeled
out for a particular occasion
work satisfactorily, and some
of the kettle barbecues (those
with a lid that closes over the
food) are inexpensive,
colourful and attractive. If you
are designing a built-in
barbecue, add a storage
cupboard if possible, and also
somewhere to place plates and
kitchen accessories. If buying a
portable barbecue, you may
wish to consider a trolley
barbecue with sufficient
surface space for serving.

■ OPPOSITE TOP

TWO-IN-ONE Almost anyone with a
barbecue will tell you that it is an
uninteresting feature when not in use.
Why not transform it into a seat?
Remove the grill and metal plate, brush
away any ash, then slot in the wooden
seat. Add a cushion, and the
transformation is comfortable and
complete.

DESIGN TIP *If you have a small garden,
make every part of it work. Look for
multi-purpose features like this barbecue
seat, or use a portable barbecue that can be
stored away when not in use.*

■ OPPOSITE BELOW

DESIGNING WITH LIGHTS Lights
positioned under a tree will cast a subtle
light for dining, as well as dramatic,
enchanting shadows.

DESIGN TIP *Consider electric lighting
at the design stage, so that it can be
planned without dangerous trailing cables.
Low-voltage systems are the safest, but
high voltage lights are more powerful and
safe if installed by an expert. However,
the cost of laying mains cable electricity
lines in conduit will be cheaper if close
to a mains supply.*

■ ABOVE

BUILT-IN BARBECUE If outdoor
entertaining is high on your list of
priorities, a built-in barbecue and seating
is worth designing into your patio. This
is an unexciting feature when the
barbecue's cold, but here a white seat
helps to enliven what could otherwise be
a drab corner once the guests have left.

DESIGN TIP *Build the barbecue in a
position that is unobtrusive when it's out
of use, and away from a fence or other
potential fire risk. For the same reason,
avoid a position near overhanging trees.*

■ TOP

CANDLES Patio lights extend the
hours of pleasure to be derived from
your patio, and allow you to enjoy warm
evenings to the full. Candles and flares
lend atmosphere to an evening in the
garden, as do lanterns.

DESIGN TIP *Position candle flares and
lanterns where their light will cast
evocative shadows around the garden.
Grouped together, they will provide
sufficient light for an atmospheric meal.
Never leave candles, flares or lanterns
unattended in the garden.*

Know-how

LOOKING DOWN

The surfacing material for a
patio is usually chosen after
the basic shape and position
have been decided, but never
overlook the relevance of this
important choice. It will
make a difference to the
image your patio creates.
Mistakes will be expensive
and hard to hide. There are
many materials from which
to choose, and dozens of
combinations to experiment
with; here are just a few.

■ OPPOSITE ABOVE

PAVERS Bricks and clay pavers are popular for small patios, and they look especially effective if combined with brick pillars and low retaining walls. Not all bricks suitable for building walls are appropriate for paving, however, so check with your supplier or use a suitable brick that's a close match.

DESIGN TIP *Terracotta pots look good with bricks or clay pavers, but try using a group of them together rather than dotting them around: this will have more impact and look less fussy.*

■ OPPOSITE BELOW

DECKING Timber decking is easy on the eye and harmonizes well with most plants. There are many decking styles, some of which are illustrated in the box above, and by using different wood stains or colours, even more effects can be created. It's advisable to experiment with a small area, or draw up a plan before buying and laying decking, to make sure that the pattern you like will suit the shape and style of your patio. Decking is also good for covering up uneven or irregular surfaces and will provide a sense of cohesion.

DESIGN TIP *Wooden furniture blends well with decking, but other materials can be used. If you are using trellis as a boundary to a decked patio, staining this a matching colour will help to produce a co-ordinated look.*

DECORATIVE DECKING

The way the planks are arranged changes the appearance of decking, as these eight variations show. Not all patterns are suitable for an irregularly shaped deck. Those that form a number of symmetrical squares are more appropriate for a rectangular deck.

If in doubt, try laying out various patterns before you cut and secure the timbers.

■ ABOVE

COMBINED EFFECTS Modern concrete-based paving materials and walling blocks mixed with brick can look pleasing and are especially useful where a modern image is desired. Don't be too tempted by brash colours, as they can look garish when new and weather to a muted colour anyway.

DESIGN TIP *Give an area of concrete paving an edging of bricks, clay pavers or tiles. It gives the paving a more definite edge and the contrast provides a clean, sharp look.*

■ LEFT

CONCRETE Don't dismiss concrete as a material. Concrete pavers can work well in the right setting. Here they blend with the concrete blocks used as seats.

DESIGN TIP *Consider how materials will blend with other features on the patio. Here, concrete blocks give the patio a modern image, but they might have looked incongruous with aluminium alloy furniture in traditional style.*

Planning and Planting
SOPHISTICATED COURTYARD

Quarry (terracotta) tiles can work better than bricks or paving slabs in a courtyard like the one shown here, as they help to create the impression of an outdoor room. A garden like this is very much an extension of the indoor living area.

PLANNING

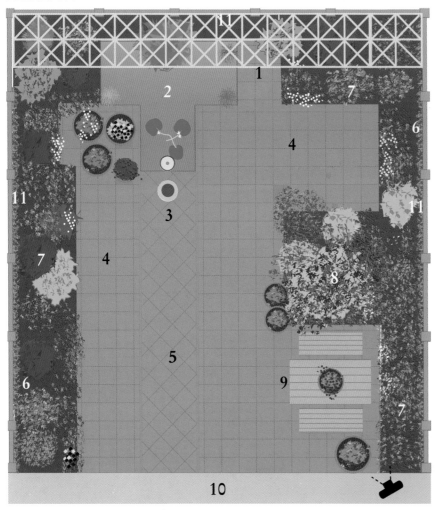

Here are instructions for building an upright trellis arbour, which can be adapted if you want to erect an overhead trellis.

CONSTRUCTING A TRELLIS ARBOUR

1 Gather together the trellis panels and "dry assemble" to ensure you are happy with the design. Two of the 200 x 60cm (6 x 2ft) panels are for the sides and the third is for the top. The two narrow panels and the concave panel are for the front and the 200 x 90cm (6 x 3ft) panel is to be used horizontally at the top of the back. Trim the wooden posts to length. They should be 200cm (6ft) plus the depth of the metal "shoe" at the top of the metal spike that will hold the post.

The type of paving used will set the tone of a patio or courtyard. These warm-looking quarry (terracotta) tiles reflect the warm-climate feel of this garden. Water plays an important role in this kind of design, but the formal pond does not have to be large, and a gentle fountain is more appropriate than a gushing water feature.

Even the most attractive paving can look overpowering if there's too much of it. Using a strip laid diagonally introduces the necessary visual break without damaging the sense of unity and harmony within the garden.

The long trellis overhead and the trellis enclosing the garden provide useful shade and a sense of privacy.

PLANTING

■ ABOVE
An upright trellis painted in a co-ordinating colour, and surrounded by colourful, fragrant plants in bed and pots, makes a perfect secluded retreat.

2 Start with the back panel. The posts need to be placed 200cm (6ft) apart. Mark their positions, then, using a club hammer, drive in a spiked metal post support (protect the top with a piece of wood or special metal insert). Drive a ready-trimmed post into each of the metal "shoes". Using the galvanized nails and the hammer, temporarily fix the top of the trellis to the top of the posts. Using a No. 8 bit, drill holes for the screws at intervals down each side of the trellis. Screw in the screws.

3 In the same way, position the front outside posts and fix the side panels, then the inside front posts and front panels. Fix the concave panel into the panels either side of it. Finally, fix the roof in position, screwing it into the posts. Paint the arbour with exterior decorative wood stain and leave to dry.

TOOLS AND MATERIALS

For a 200cm (6ft) long trellis:
Lattice (diagonal) trellis in the
   following panels:
   3 panels 200 x 60cm
   (6 x 2ft)
   2 panels 200 x 30cm
   (6 x 1ft)
   1 concave panel 200 x 45cm
   (6 x 1½ft)
   1 panel 200 x 90cm (6 x 3ft)
   6 timber posts 8 x 8cm
   (3 x 3in), each 2.2m (7ft)
Saw
6 spiked metal post supports
   8 x 8cm(3 x 3in), each 75cm
   (2½ft) long
Club hammer
10 x 5cm (2in) galvanized nails
Hammer
Electric drill with No. 8 bit,
   screwdriver attachment
40 x 2.5cm (1in) No. 10 zinc-
   coated steel screws
2.5 litre (½ gallon) can exterior
   woodstain
Small decorating brush

Planning and Planting
SURROUNDED BY FRAGRANCE

Instead of making your patio formal and structural, try building it into the edge of a border. You will feel more immersed in your garden, and if you use plenty of scented plants it will be a wonderfully fragrant experience too.

PLANNING

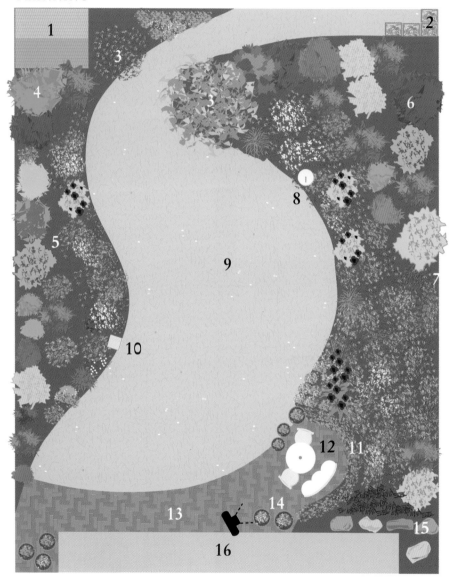

will enhance the aromatic delights of sitting in this enchanting part of the garden. Bear in mind that these aromatic plants will also attract lots of bees, which could be an inconvenience.

SITTING PRETTY
Instead of buying garden furniture, you could give some old tables and chairs a lick of paint, and you may be able to colour co-ordinate them with the surrounding plants. Wooden furniture will look best. You can be sure of perfect toning as paints are available in hundreds of shades. If you don't have any suitable old chairs, try junk shops. To maintain the chairs in good condition, keep them indoors when not required outside.

If the formality of a rectangular patio conventionally positioned by the house does not appeal to you, and you want your sitting area integrated more naturally into an informal garden style, try building a small sitting area into one of the borders.

The bank of thyme surrounding the seating area will be fragrant when touched or the leaves are crushed, and the pots of lavender

PLANTING

■ ABOVE
These bright Caribbean colours may not harmonize with many plants, but your garden certainly won't be dull with a chair like this.

■ ABOVE
A combination of grey and white looks cool and elegant and will blend with most garden settings. Natural or muted colours contrast well with the bright blooms of seasonal flowers.

■ ABOVE
Prettily decorated with the bright colours typical of a summer garden, this chair would look wonderful surrounded by bright bedding plants such as fiery red pelargoniums.

■ ABOVE
The chair shown above blends in sympathetically with the painted shed behind. The delight of this project is that you can choose shades and colours to blend or contrast.

Planning and Planting
ON THE ROOF

Roof gardens have limited scope for radical overhauls as structural and load-bearing considerations will determine the scope. Furniture and plants are elements that will set the style.

PLANNING

Roof gardens offer more scope than balconies as they are often larger, but the problems are the same. The physical structure dictates the basic shape and limits of what you can do. Choose furniture and plants carefully to evoke atmosphere. Here, a formal garden has been created with box and other "architectural" evergreens in a simple planting scheme. These shrubs tolerate the winds more readily than less robust plants.

This roof is able to take the weight of the numerous clay pots, but with other roof gardens it may be necessary to use plastic containers and lightweight potting soil. Make sure they are heavy enough to withstand severe winds. If in doubt about your roof's load-bearing capacity, consult a structural engineer.

CLASSIC TOPIARY
Topiary is easy to maintain. When trimming, don't get carried away. Little and often with an ordinary pair of scissors is better than the occasional dramatic gesture with a pair of shears.

PLANTING

■ **BELOW**
left to right:
Ball topiary, corkscrew topiary, three-ball topiary and classic standard ball topiary. With patience and skill, box topiary can be trained from young plants. Buying ready-trained specimens will create instant impact.

POTTING TOPIARY

1 Knock the plant out of its original pot. Place into the terracotta pot containing broken crocks, and fill the space around the rootball with potting soil.

2 Push the potting soil down the side of the pot firmly, to ensure that there are no air spaces. Scatter the surface of the soil with plant food and water well.

3 To conserve moisture and create an elegant finish, especially on standard topiaries, cover the top with a generous layer of chipped bark or gravel.

Planning and Planting
CENTRE OF ATTRACTION

Your patio or sitting area will probably have far more character if you break with tradition and move it to a more central position, away from the house. A patio like this places you at the heart of the garden where you can admire the view.

PLANNING

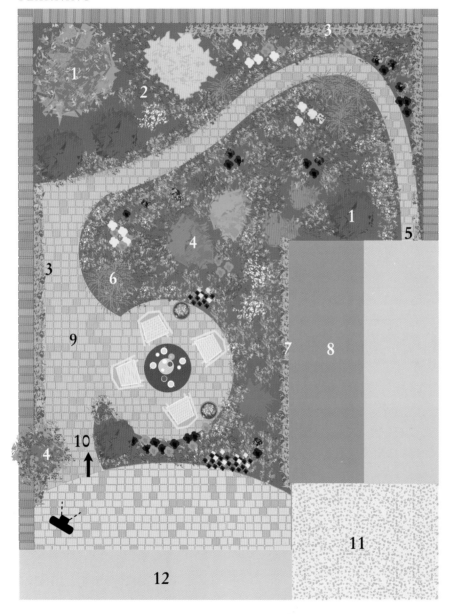

KEY TO PLAN

1 Specimen tree
2 Mixed border
3 Climbers on wall
4 Specimen shrubs
5 Rear door to garage
6 Mixed planting
7 Climbers on garage wall
8 Garage
9 Granite setts
10 Granite sett steps
11 Drive
12 House

↑ Direction of steps down

Viewpoint on photograph

The structure of this garden does not follow any of the common grids based on rectangles or series of circles, which amply demonstrates that design "rules" should be interpreted flexibly. Some of the best gardens give the impression of having simply evolved, with one part melting into the next. Curves and straight lines do not usually mix happily, however, and this garden is full of circles, arcs and gentle curves.

SITTING COMFORTABLY
Garden seats should be practical as well as pretty whenever possible. Charming and elegant seats are available in practical cast-aluminium alloy (they look like wrought iron from a distance, but are much lighter and more practical for use outdoors), but even old seats from around the garden and home can sometimes be renovated and used to give your garden character.

It is the clever use of meandering paths of granite setts combined with masses of plants that make this tasteful garden a delight for the plant enthusiast. Positioning the main sitting area slightly away from the house, so that it is surrounded by shrubs and mixed planting, makes it a magical place to sit and have a meal.

PLANTING

■ RIGHT
The old Lloyd
loom chair
illustrated had
been given a new
look a few years
earlier with two
shades of blue
spray-on car
paint. Even
though the finish
has become worn,
the chair exudes a
comfortable,
cottage-garden
feel. This kind of
chair is not really
weatherproof, but
it can sit in a
conservatory and
be brought out
for special
occasions.

■ ABOVE
Metal benches are often unattractive, but
this one was given a new lease of life
when it was painted a bright
Mediterranean blue. Used with a couple
of co-ordinated cushions, it would add
charm to any sitting area.

Planning and Planting
ELEGANT FORMALITY

Even city gardens like this one offer scope for a sense of spacious elegance, combining a long, open view to a distant focal point with plenty of interest-packed areas of restrained formality.

PLANNING

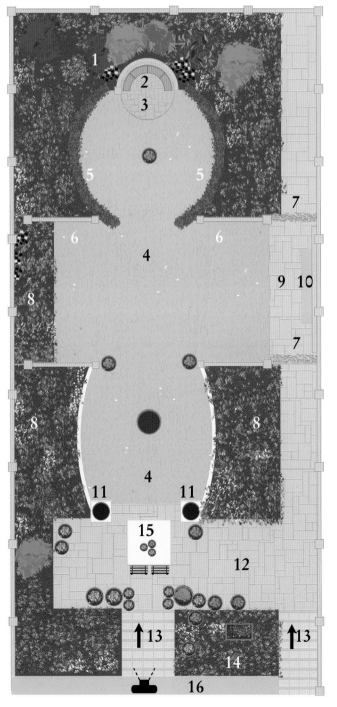

KEY TO PLAN

1	Shrub border		seating area
2	Curved trellis with seat	10	Trellis arbour
3	Circular paved area	11	Urn
4	Lawn	12	Random-slab patio
5	Box (*Buxus sempervirens*) hedge	13	Steps
6	Downcurving trellis with climbers	14	Dwarf shrubs
7	Archway with climber	15	Seating area
8	Mixed border	16	House
9	Random-slab	↑	Direction of steps up
			Viewpoint on photograph

A design with many interesting features, this garden illustrates how effectively a simple device like a trellis can break up the garden visually. Shaped trellises have been used to divide the garden into a series of compartments. A trellis adds height and structure without blocking the view or casting a heavy shadow in the way that a hedge or wall does. Trellises can also be painted or stained in various colours to create a particular mood or emphasize a style.

It's possible to buy ready-made shaped trellises from specialist suppliers, but they can also be made to suit a specific need.

The curved trellis at the end of the garden encloses a small sitting area, something that balances the patio at the house end of the garden and also provides a focal point. It's a good idea to have more than one patio, so that you always have a sunny place to sit as the sun moves around. The secondary sitting area does not have to be large. This kind of design is easily achieved without a great deal of construction if there is already an existing central lawn.

PLANTING CLIMBERS
Trellises of all kinds, whether grand like the ones shown in the picture above or modest and erected specifically for a climber, demand to be clothed. It's not necessary to cover the whole trellis with climbers (sometimes the exposed structure strengthens the sense of design), but a good degree of cover avoids it looking too bare.

If the trellis is close to a wall or fence, it's very important to plant a little distance away, to avoid the worst of the "rain shadow".

PLANTING

PLANTING A CLIMBER

1 Excavate a hole twice the diameter of the rootball. The centre of the plant should be 30cm (1ft) away from the wall or fence, otherwise the roots will be too dry. Dig in a generous amount of rotted manure or garden compost, to help hold moisture in the soil as well as add nutrients.

2 Water the plant, then gently knock the bottom of the container to remove the plant from its original pot. Carefully tease out some of the fine roots from around the edge of the rootball, to encourage them to grow into the surrounding soil. Return the soil to the hole and firm.

3 Loosen the stems if they have been tied to a support cane in their pot, and spread them out evenly, spreading them wide and low. Tie in.

4 Water thoroughly after planting, and continue to water carefully until established. Apply a mulch to reduce water loss and suppress weeds.

Planning and Planting
OUTDOOR ENTERTAINING

This garden is clearly designed for the whole family to enjoy the great outdoors in the garden. There are plenty of seats for family and friends, a built-in barbecue, and a sand pit for youngsters. There's also plenty of space to play in this safe and enclosed environment.

PLANNING

KEY TO PLAN

1 Wall, painted white
2 Wall, with climbers
3 Dwarf shrubs
4 Metal arch for climbers
5 Garden bench
6 Brick paving
7 Steps
8 Barbecue with brick shelves on each side
9 Sandpit
10 Shrubs
11 Timber rail
12 Brick terrace
13 House

↑ Direction of steps up

↖ Viewpoint on photograph

This garden shows many design elements that guarantee impact: changes of level, a choice of areas for sitting and relaxing, attractive paving that harmonizes with the walls, some strong focal points, and a symmetry of construction that suggests good design.

It may seem strange that a sandpit should become a focal point, but when its usefulness as a sandpit is over, and young children have grown up, it can be turned into an attractive circular pond, perhaps with a fountain to bring movement and relaxing sounds to the scene.

LIGHTING UP
Garden lighting can be enchanting and atmospheric, and it can even make your garden a safer place if potentially hazardous steps are illuminated. If you are considering installing a high-voltage system, you should always consult a qualified electrician. A low-voltage system, however, is a relatively simple do-it-yourself job, but take professional advice, if in doubt.

PLANTING

GARDEN LIGHTING

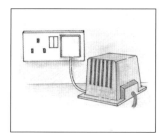

1 A low-voltage lighting kit will come with a transformer. This must always be protected from the weather, positioned in a dry place indoors or in a garage or outbuilding.

2 Using an electric drill, make a hole through the window frame or wall, just wide enough to take the cable. Fill in any gaps afterwards, using a mastic or other waterproof filler.

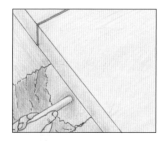

3 Although the cable carries a low voltage, it is still a potential hazard if left uncovered. Unless the lights are positioned close to where the cable emerges, run it underground in a conduit.

4 Most low-voltage lighting systems are designed to be moved around. Many of them can be pushed conveniently into the ground wherever you choose to use them.

Planning and Planting
SIMPLE ELEGANCE

Often simple shapes well executed have the most impact. This garden is based on rectangles around a large lawn. The patio is situated a distance from the house, linked by herringbone paving, which gives it a strong "architectural" element.

PLANNING

KEY TO PLAN

1 Hedge
2 Compost area
3 Shed
4 Gravel path
5 Specimen tree
6 Mixed border
7 Pergola on brick piers
8 Brick patio
9 Climbers over pergola
10 Lawn
11 Brick-edged pond
12 Brick path
13 Small specimen tree
14 Dwarf shrubs
15 Brick paving
16 House

↖ Viewpoint on photograph

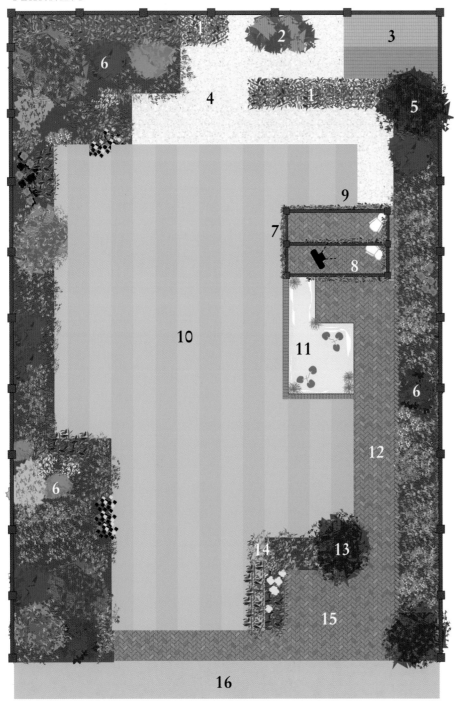

The choice of materials as well as the basic shape of the garden helps to create a sense of unity. In this garden, brick has been used extensively to link the various parts, and particularly the house and patio. Brick pillars for the patio overhead continue the theme and make the feature a more substantial element in the overall design.

Lighting has been built into the pillars as part of the patio lighting, to make this an area of the garden to be enjoyed for relaxing or dining after dusk as well as by day.

LAYING CLAY OR CONCRETE PAVERS
Bricks are usually bedded on mortar with mortared joints, but clay or concrete pavers are bedded directly on to sand. Their dimensions ensure they lock together simply by vibrating or tamping sand between them. They can be used instead of bricks, for patios or paths.

PLANTING

HOW TO LAY CLAY OR CONCRETE PAVERS

1 Excavate the area and prepare a sub-base of about 5cm (2in) of compacted hardcore or sand-and-gravel mix. Set an edging along one end and side first. Check that it's level, then mortar it into position, and lay the pavers.

2 Lay a 5cm (2in) bed of sharp sand over the area, then use a straight-edged piece of wood between two height gauges, notched at the ends so the wood strikes off surplus sand and provides a level surface.

3 Position the pavers in your chosen design, laying about 2m (6ft) at a time. Make sure they butt up to each other tightly, and are firm against the edging. Mortar further edging strips into place as you proceed.

4 Hire a flat-plate vibrator to consolidate the sand. Alternatively, tamp the pavers down with a club hammer used over a piece of wood. To avoid damage do not go too close to an unsupported edge with the vibrator.

5 Brush loose sand into the joints of the pavers with a broom, then vibrate or tamp again. It may be necessary to repeat the vibrating process once more for a firm, neat finish. The patio should be ready to use straightaway.

Planning and Planting
AN ENCHANTED JUNGLE

This dense, lush garden has both sophistication for grown-ups and drama and adventure for children, with changes of level and lots of tall, leafy plants, including a banana plant, bedded out for the summer. This plan is perfect for dining and playing.

PLANNING

Even a small area can look densely planted if you envelop your sitting area with a living screen of well-chosen plants. Changing levels and using shrubs to obscure the various sections of the garden also help to make it an exciting garden to explore and play in.

The choice of decking in this design helps to create a jungle-like atmosphere as it blends in perfectly with the plants, having a natural affinity with them.

The lower paved area acts as a practical bridge between home and the plant-filled area, and it is here that the barbecue has been situated, leaving the eating area free of anything that would detract from its natural-looking setting.

GIANT FOLIAGE PLANTS
An impressive banana plant has been used as a focal-point foliage plant in the garden photographed opposite, but such exotic plants need to be over-wintered in a conservatory or a large greenhouse if you live where temperatures drop to freezing. There are many hardy foliage plants with big or

PLANNING

bold leaves, however, and a clump of them can create the impression of lush, tropical growth.

The plants in the illustration all prefer moist soil, such as that found in a bog garden, but you can grow them in a normal bed or border if you use a trickle irrigation hose to ensure adequate moisture. Where conditions suit, the gunnera leaves can grow to 1.8m (6ft) across on stems up to 3m (10ft) tall, though in dry conditions they will be probably be smaller.

GIANT FOLIAGE PLANTS

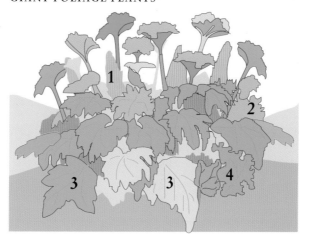

KEY TO PLANTS
....

1 *Gunnera manicata*
2 *Petasites japonicus giganteus*
3 *Rheum undulatum*
4 *Rheum palmatum tanguticum*

Planning and Planting
A SECRET GARDEN

This garden has lots of features packed into a modest-sized plot, marrying an area of lawn for relaxation and play with paving, plenty of screening and a sense of seclusion.

PLANNING

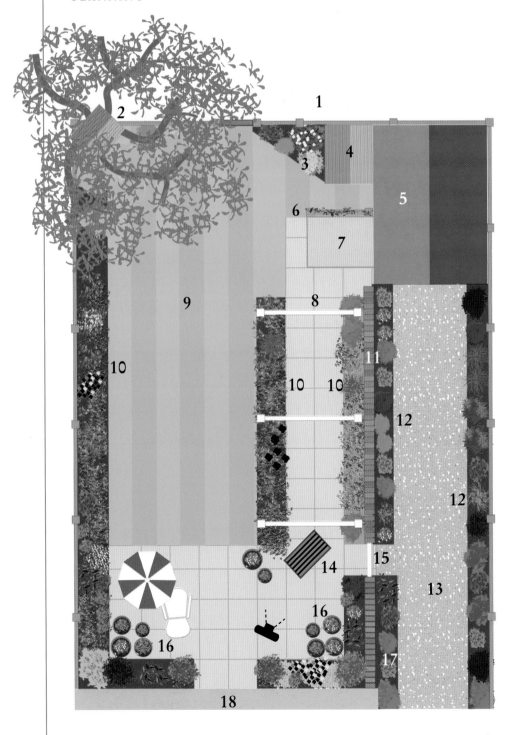

KEY TO PLAN

1 Woodland
2 Tree house
3 Shrubs
4 Shed
5 Garage
6 Climber-covered trellis
7 Sandpit
8 Pergola
9 Lawn
10 Mixed border
11 Wall
12 Ground-cover shrubs
13 Drive
14 Barbecue
15 Door to drive
16 Patios with containers
17 Dwarf shrubs
18 House

↙ Viewpoint in photograph

Children have been well catered for in this garden, with a sandpit and a tree house, together with a lawn where the whole family can play and relax. The pergola gives shade and a sense of seclusion, and it ensures that the garden has height and a sense of structure. A trellis positioned behind the sandpit helps to screen the garden shed from view.

A garage and drive can dominate a garden if not screened. Here a dividing wall solves the problem by disguising the drive. If building a brick wall seems a daunting job, screen (pierced) walling blocks are easy to lay and will still act as a screen, especially if climbers or shrubs are used to clothe them.

LIGHTWEIGHT PERGOLAS
The strongest pergolas are made from sawn wood (lumber), but a lightweight structure can be easily constructed from rustic poles and will blend in with the surroundings effectively.

PLANTING

HOW TO JOIN RUSTIC POLES

1 Using a handsaw, saw a notch of suitable size at the top of the upright post to take a horizontal piece of wood snugly.

2 Where two rails have to be joined, do this over an upright. Cut matching notches so that one piece sits directly over the other.

3 To fix cross-pieces to horizontals, cut a V-shaped notch into the crosspiece, using a chisel if necessary, then nail into place.

4 Use halving joints where two pieces cross. Make two saw cuts halfway through the pole, then chisel out the waste. Use a wood adhesive and secure a halving joint with a nail for extra strength.

5 Bird's-mouth joints are useful for connecting horizontal and diagonal pieces to uprights. Remove a V-shaped notch about 2.5cm (1in) deep, then saw the other piece to match. Use a chisel to achieve a good fit.

Choosing Plants

PATIO, BALCONY AND ROOF GARDEN PLANTS

The majority of plants can be grown in pots. Use shrubby and annual climbers to clothe patio walls, and a few striking "architectural" shrubby plants as focal points, but make the most of bedding plants, tender perennials and containers for masses of summer colour.

CLIMBERS AND WALL SHRUBS

Patios and balconies almost always have a wall boundary on at least one side, which would be more attractive if clothed with attractive climbers or wall shrubs. Ivies are ideal for clothing a large wall, but try to include plants with flowers or attractive berries to make it more interesting. Large-flowered clematis are ideal if supported on a trellis, but avoid rampant ones such as *C. montana*. Avoid thorny climbing or rambling roses if the space is confined. Pyracanthas are ideal wall shrubs as they can be trained and confined easily.

Clematis Large-flowered clematis are among the most popular and spectacular climbers to grow up a trellis. These varieties are 'Nelly Moser' (top) and 'Lasurstern' (bottom), but garden centres will have many to choose from.

"ARCHITECTURAL" SHRUBS

These are plants with a strong profile such as a spiky appearance or large bold leaves, which act as a focal point or a clearly defined shape. Avoid plants with spine-tipped leaves, such as *Yucca gloriosa* for example, as these can be dangerous, especially for children. *Cordyline australis* has a spiky appearance but softer tips, and there are prettily variegated varieties. Phormiums make striking plants for beds or large containers, and are available with variegated and coloured leaves.

Cordyline australis 'Albertii' is one of several variegated forms of this architectural plant, useful as a focal point. It is likely to be less hardy than the all-green species, so it may require winter protection in cold areas.

BORDER PLANTS FOR CONTAINERS

Few border plants are used in containers other than hostas, but it's worth experimenting if you have spare pieces of border plants left over when you divide them. Because they are not usually grown in containers, the impact of potted border plants can be greater. *Lychnis coronaria* can be very pleasing, and *Ligularia dentata*

Hostas come in many forms. Most are attractively variegated, and some have pleasant flowers. They do surprisingly well in containers if watered regularly. This makes them highly desirable foliage plants for a patio.

'Desdemona' can be impressive with its large, almost purple leaves. Generally, foliage plants are a better choice than those grown mainly for flowers.

TREES AND SHRUBS FOR CONTAINERS

Patio colour is usually provided by summer-flowering seasonal plants, but it's worth growing a few evergreen shrubs in large containers, so that your patio or balcony does not look too bleak in winter. *Viburnum tinus* is especially useful because it flowers all winter. *Fatsia japonica* is grown mainly for its striking foliage, but mature plants do have ball-like heads of whitish flowers in late autumn. Small trees such as laburnums and some acers can be grown successfully in large pots.

PATIO ROSES

Most roses can be grown in large containers, but they will be much happier in beds beside the patio or cut into a patio. There are, however, patio roses – really dwarf and compact floribunda (cluster-flowered) varieties – that perform well in pots and in patio beds. 'Sweet Dream' and 'Top Marks' are particularly good, but there are many more.

Patio roses do best in flowerbeds or raised beds on the patio, but will usually put on a respectable performance in a container too. This one is 'Top Marks', one of the most highly regarded varieties among professional rose growers.

POPULAR BEDDING PLANTS

Any of the popular bedding plants can be used in patio containers, and which you grow is purely a matter of personal preference. Pelargoniums (bedding geraniums) should be on the short list, however, because they have that Mediterranean look and thrive in a hot position. They are also less demanding regarding watering than most other bedding plants. Busy Lizzies (impatiens) are also priority patio plants because they

Trailing pelargoniums, with their bright, vigorous blooms, can be used to great effect in both window boxes and hanging baskets. They are particularly good plants for containers as they will tolerate a period of dry soil better than most plants.

are so long-flowering and tolerate shade or sun. The New Guinea hybrids, which have larger flowers and sometimes variegated leaves, are not generally used for mass bedding, but they make excellent patio plants.

INTERESTING TENDER PERENNIALS

The group of brightly coloured summer flowers loosely called tender perennials, to distinguish them from bedding plants raised from seeds, are always worth including. They have to be propagated vegetatively and overwintered in a frost-free place, so if you don't have a greenhouse it's usually necessary to buy fresh plants each year. Fuchsias are a popular example, but try some of the bright daisy-like plants too, as these suggest a warm climate. Argyranthemums, venidioarctotis, and osteospermums are good examples and will continue flowering over a long period.

Argyranthemum frutescens is probably still better known as *Chrysanthemum frutescens*. There are many varieties with daisy-like flowers in shades of pink, yellow and white, produced over a long period. This is is 'Sharpitor'.

A TOUCH OF THE EXOTIC

A sheltered patio or balcony may provide the right environment for some of the plants more usually grown in a greenhouse or conservatory, where winters are frosty. Coleus are easily raised from seed, so can be discarded at the end of the season. Try putting some of your houseplants on the patio for the summer, after careful hardening off (acclimatizing).

Coleus are often grown as pot plants, but they can be grown very successfully in the garden. They are easy to raise from seed, started into growth in warmth in mid or late winter.

INDEX

The page numbers in *italics* refer to illustrations.

Acer 92
    A. griseum 58
Ajuga reptans
        'Atropurpurea' 59
aluminium chairs 67, *67*
angular corner gardens
    21, *21*
arbours 74–5, *74, 75*
arches 43, *43*
architectural plants 78, 92
Argyranthemum
        frutescens 93, *93*
aromatic plants *see*
    scented plants

balconies 62, 65, 92–3
banana plant 88, *89*
barbecues 39, *39*, 70
    built-in *71*
    portable 71
basement gardens 44–5,
    44, 45
bedding plants 93, *93*
benches 67, *81*
bergenia 59
birch 56
borders
    built-up 42, *42*
    plants 59, 92
boundaries 26, *26*, 36–7,
    36, 37
box hedge *see Buxus*
    sempervirens
bricks *86, 87*
    patios *73*
    raised beds 45
Busy Lizzies 93
Buxus sempervirens 33,
    78, 79

cacti *62*
candles *71*
cane furniture *67*
cast-iron furniture 67
cavity walls 37, *37*
chairs *87*
    aluminium 67, *67*
    fold-away *66*
    Lloyd loom *81*
    natural materials *67*
    wooden 66, *67*, 76, *77*
    see also sitting areas
Chamaecyparis pisifera
    'Filifera Aurea' 58

chamomile 23
children 84, 90
circular themes 16, *16,*
    20, 20, 56, 56, 57
clay pavers *73*, 86, 87,
    87
Clematis 37, 92, 93
climbing plants 37, 43,
    43, 82, 83, 83, 92
clothes driers 38, *38*
coleus 93, *93*
colour 33
concrete pavers *73,* 86,
    87, *87*
conifers 58
containers
    border plants 92
    focal points 54, *55*
    trees and shrubs 92
Cordyline australis 47, 92,
    92
corner gardens 21, *21*
cornering 56–7
Corsican mint lawn 52,
    53, *53*
Cotoneaster horizontalis
    59
cottage-style gardens *8,*
    24, *24, 25, 31,* 35
courtyards 74–5
Crataegus oxyacantha 58
Cupressus macrocarpa
    'Goldcrest' 58, *58*
curved corner gardens
    21, *21*

deciduous shrubs 59
deciduous trees 58
decking, timber *73,* 88,
    88, 89
design 14–15, 31–59
diagonal themes 16, *17*
doors 40, *40*
doronicum 59, *59*
drains 39, *39*
drawing 12–13
Drimys winteri 58, *58*
driveways 24–5
dustbin 39, *39*
dwarf conifers 58

edging
    sawn log *55*
    Victorian style rope
        54, *55*
    wavy-edged *55*
endless paths 41, *41*
Erica carnea 59
Euonymus fortunei 43
evergreen oak *see*
    Quercus ilex
evergreen planting 46,
    46
evergreen shrubs 58–9,
    59, 92
evergreen trees 58
exotic plants 93, *93*

Fatsia japonica 92
fences
    as features 36, *36*

living 37, *37*
    picket 36, *36*
    preservation 36
    windows 36, *36*
focal points 21, 54–5, *54,*
    55, 56
fold-away chairs 66
formal gardens 18, *18*
front gardens 24–5
furniture 66–7, *66, 67*
    comfortable 80
    permanent *68*
    white painted *64*
    wicker *68*
    wooden *66, 67, 73,*
        76, 77
    see also chairs
Fuchia 47, 93

gates 40
gazebos *33*
geometry 20–1, 52–3
geranium 93, *93*
giant foliage plants 88–9,
    89
gravel 56, 57, *57,* 62
grid approach 14–15
Gunnera manicata 89, *89*

hawthorn 58, *58*
heather 59
Hebe × franciscana
    'Variegata' 59
holly 58
hosta 92, *92*
Hydrangea macrophylla
    59

illusions 26–7, 40–1
impatiens 93
informal gardens 19, *19*
inspiration 14, 32–5

Japanese-style gardens
    32, 33
joist hanger 51
Juniperus
    J. communis
        'Hibernica' 58
    J. scopulorum
        'Skyrocket' 58
    J. squamata
        'Blue Star' 58

L-shaped gardens 21, *21*
laburnum 92
lavender 76
lawns

ACKNOWLEDGEMENTS

The author and publisher are grateful to acknowledge the work of Robert Crawford Clarke, who has kindly extrapolated the plans for the gardens. These plans do not necessarily reflect the original designer's plan. Where known, the existing garden designers are acknowledged below.

t = top, b = bottom, l = left, r = right, m = middle

A-Z Botanical Collection Ltd: p67tr Sylvia O'Toole; p77tl Mike Vardy; p34 James Braidwood; p35t Adrian Thomas (design by Wendy Bundy).

Pat Brindley: p35b.

Jonathan Buckley: p83t; p29b; p30; p51.

The Garden Picture Library: p7 Gil Hanly (Nan Raymond Garden, New Zealand); p8 Gil Hanly (Ethidge Gardens, Timaru, Canterbury, New Zealand, Nan and Wynne Raymond); p19 Gil Hanly (Penny Zino Garden, Flaxmere, Hawarden, New Zealand); p60 J.S Sira (Chelsea Flower Show, London); p61 Brigitte Thomas; p62t Jerry Pavia; p62b Ron Sutherland; p63 Henk Dijkman; p64 Steven Wooster; p65t Marijke Heuff; p65b Ron Sutherland (John Zerning Balcony); p66bl Friedrich Strauss; p70 Ron Sutherland (Anthony Paul Design); p75tl Ron Sutherland (Eco Design, Melbourne, Australia); p79t Ron Sutherland (Anthony Paul Design); p81 Brigitte Thomas; p32b Ron Sutherland (Paul Flemming Design, Melbourne, Australia); p33 Gil Hanley (Bruce Cornish Garden, Auckland); p47bl John Glover; p57t Marianne Majerus (John Brooks Design, BBC Garden); p85 Ron Sutherland (Michael Balston Design); p89 Ron Sutherland (Godfrey Amy's Garden, Jersey, Anthony Paul Design); p91t David Askham.

Robert Harding Picture Library: p68t Ian Baldwin Pool; p49t James Merrell; p53b BBC Enterprises/Redwood Publishing (design by Jean Bishop).

Andrew Lawson Photographic: p31.

Peter McHoy: p9 (David Sandford); p23 ; p25; p67tr (design by Kathleen McHoy), bl; p68; p69; p70t; p71b; p72; p73; p87t; p92tr; p92br; p93; p32t (design by Jean Bishop); p36b; p37b; p38; p39; p40l; p41b; p43l, bl; p58t,c,b; p59.

Harry Smith Horticultural Collection: p26.